ONCE A SOLDIER, TWICE A PIONEER

Joshua Hobbs Brown: The Story of an American Hero

STEVE GRASZ

authorHOUSE®

AuthorHouse™
1663 Liberty Drive
Bloomington, IN 47403
www.authorhouse.com
Phone: 833-262-8899

Published by AuthorHouse 01/15/2021

ISBN: 978-1-6655-1209-1 (sc)
ISBN: 978-1-6655-1207-7 (hc)
ISBN: 978-1-6655-1208-4 (e)

Library of Congress Control Number: 2020925653

Print information available on the last page.

Cover image: Battle of Stones River, Kurz and Allison,
Art Publishers, Chicago, 1891. Library of Congress.

This book is printed on acid-free paper.

Dedication

This book is dedicated to all those in my family who have served our country in uniform and to those who have farmed the land, including my parents. I want to thank my beautiful wife, Verlyne, and my children; Caylen and Jerrold, Nate and Brenna, Jackson, and Aubrey for their love and support.

I learned a great deal about my family, about the hardships of war and homesteading, and even about myself while writing this book. I will always treasure my research trips to Chappell, Nebraska and Aledo, Illinois as well as to Homestead National Monument, Stones River National Battlefield, Arlington National Cemetery, and Nashville. I hold an even deeper appreciation for my forebearers and their many sacrifices to preserve our union and to settle the vast prairies.

In a hand-written letter (circa 1975) intended to help preserve details of the family history, Joshua Brown's granddaughter, Mary LaSelle Jankovsky (my maternal grandmother), wrote, "When I think of Grandpa (Joshua H) and my grandmother [Mary], I believe someone should write a book. Their lives were so eventful—Civil War, pioneers, 1st Clydesdales brought to Deuel County, etc." I re-discovered this 45-year-old letter while researching for this book, and I am happy to fulfill my grandmother's wish.

I want to express my gratitude to the many who assisted with the research necessary to tell the story of Joshua Hobbs Brown: the Chappell Memorial Library and Art Gallery (Chappell, Nebraska); the Mercer County Historical Society and Essley Noble Museum (Aledo, Illinois); Lois Retherford of Aledo, Illinois; Homestead National Monument (Beatrice, Nebraska); Huntsville-Madison County Public Library (Huntsville, Alabama); Mercer County Illinois Sheriff's Office; Deuel County Nebraska Clerk's Office; Mercer County Illinois Clerk's Office; the Cheyenne County Historical Society (Sidney, Nebraska); the *Chappell Register*; Jerrold Warren Photography; and my grandmother for preserving and passing on the stories of an American hero named Joshua Brown.

CONTENTS

Joshua Hobbs Brown and Mary Dilley Brown, circa 1870.
Photo restoration by Jerrold Warren Photography.

"One generation will commend Your works to the next and will proclaim Your mighty acts." [1]

CHAPTER ONE

Prairie State Pioneer

JOSHUA HOBBS BROWN WAS ONCE a solider and twice a pioneer. He is forever an American hero. It is rare for any man or woman to be at the center of a history-altering event or to help found a new civilization from the ground up—let alone to do so twice. But Joshua Brown did all of this. He fought valiantly to save the Union during the darkest hours of the American Civil War and to free millions of enslaved human beings in the process. Joshua was seriously wounded on the battlefield but survived to fight on in many of the most famous battles of the war. He helped settle not one, but two states as a pioneer: first in the earliest days of the settlement of the prairies of Western Illinois and then in the first years of settling the high plains of Western Nebraska.

Joshua's pioneering spirit and his battlefield bravery likely came from his character-shaping childhood and youth on the Illinois frontier. While many know the state of Illinois as the "Land of Lincoln," its original—and still official—nickname is actually "The Prairie State." Long after statehood in 1818, much of Illinois remained wild native prairie. The area bordering the Mississippi River in Western Illinois[2], in what is now Mercer County, was home to the Sauk[3] and Fox Indian tribes and the prairie sod was yet to be broken by the plows and determination of hardy pioneers.

As students of history know, Illinois's most famous figure, Abraham Lincoln, was born in a log cabin in rural LaRue County Kentucky on February 12th, 1809. The following year, in neighboring Nelson County, Kentucky, a boy named Benjamin Franklin Brown was born on April 7th— almost certainly in a log cabin as well—to Samuel and Henrietta (Hobbs) Brown. Lincoln eventually moved to the Illinois prairie with his family in

1

1830. The next year, Benjamin Franklin Brown moved to the Illinois prairie with his mother and most of his siblings following the death of his father. Henrietta and six of the Brown children eventually settled in Knox County while Benjamin and his brothers, Harison and John H., settled nearby in what would become Mercer County. Benjamin was, in fact, "[a]mong the earliest settlers" in North Henderson Township in 1831.[4]

This was the very beginning of what would become a historic transformation of the region. Native Americans, who had begun losing what remained of their Illinois lands, decided to make a stand against the encroaching settlers. Led by Chief Black Hawk, a 65-year-old member of the Sauk tribe, 500 warriors and an equal number of women and children from several tribes crossed the Mississippi River back into Illinois from neighboring Iowa. They hoped to reclaim their former lands. This alarmed the sparsely populated pioneer settlements. Only six families with a total of 26 people lived in the Mercer County area.[5] By themselves, they would have been no match for 500 warriors. However, numerous frontier settlements banded together for protection, and a militia force was raised in the state that eventually numbered in the thousands.

Benjamin Brown was among the volunteers. Stepping forward to protect his family and his new home, he promptly joined Captain William McMurty's mounted ranger company of the Illinois militia in the spring of 1832.[6] The Company consisted of 70-90 men on horses. This was basically all the able-bodied men in the area. That same spring, young Abe Lincoln also joined the militia and was selected to lead his Company during what would become known as the Black Hawk War. He served from April 21st to June 10th, 1832. On one excursion Lincoln led his Company through the future Mercer County. It is not known whether Abe and Benjamin crossed paths. Little did Benjamin know that one day his own son would serve the country in another much larger war, led by Lincoln.

The Black Hawk War was short-lived, and hostilities soon ceased. But life on the frontier was not easy. To make ends meet, Benjamin left his brothers to work in the lead mines around Galena, Illinois in 1833 and 1834, about one hundred miles to the north. In the spring of 1835, he returned and began to make improvements on a land claim. Now that the Black Hawk War was over, more pioneer families felt safe to settle in the area and the time arrived to establish a local government. On January 1st, 1835, Mercer County, Illinois was officially formed.[7]

In 1836, Benjamin sold his land interest in Mercer County to his brother, Harison,[8] and joined the rest of his family in nearby Knox County. However, he would not be gone long. On February 2nd, 1838, Benjamin married Miss Lucinda Mann. This was the very first marriage recorded in North Henderson Township in Mercer County.[9] Together, Benjamin and Lucinda began to improve a land claim on sections 6 and 7, building a "traditional log cabin."[10] Because there were no roads, railroads, or other practical ways to get lumber for construction, Benjamin chose a location with both open prairie land suitable for farming and wooded creek bottomland to be used as a "timber lot."[11] This homestead became the heart of their budding farm. Before long, Benjamin and Lucinda had started a family. On July 6th, 1841, there in North Henderson Township, Lucinda gave birth to Joshua Hobbs Brown.[12] Joshua was the second of seven children and the first boy. His safe birth was a true blessing, as during Lucinda's pregnancy a Scarlet Fever epidemic swept the small pioneer community. In a single month in 1840, ten of the Brown's neighbors perished. All were buried just east of Benjamin and Lucinda's farmstead in what would become the Mann Cemetery.[13]

Joshua grew up knowing the wonders of nature, the freedom of self-determination, and the hardships of breaking the thick prairie sod to scratch out a living. He worked the land as well as hunted and fished to contribute to the table. For years, Joshua farmed alongside his family, transforming the wild prairie into some of America's best and most productive farmland. Daily life for Joshua consisted largely of physical labor without benefit of technology beyond horse-drawn single blade plows. In fact, it was not until 1837—just four years before Joshua's birth—when a man named John Deere manufactured the first commercially successful cast-steel plow just over 100 miles away in Grand Detour, Illinois.[14]

In addition to hard work, his parents stressed education, and Joshua received schooling in the North Henderson public schools.[15] A small country schoolhouse was located just a short walk from the Brown's cabin. This was by no means typical in that day. As surprising as it may seem now, public schools were a new thing in the United States and were even more rare and remarkable in frontier areas. Although Joshua would never have the chance to attend college, he would carry on the heritage of valuing education and it would impact generations of his descendants.

Joshua's stamina-building work on the family farm, as well as his ability to build with his own hands, use a rifle, and survive in a world with no modern comforts or conveniences would later serve him well in ways he never could have imagined in those early years. For now, though, there was much to be done. Joshua and his family did not just start a farm. They formed a county and established a community with churches, schools, businesses, and local government. They built a civilization from the ground up. This alone would be historic. But Joshua was just getting started.

CHAPTER TWO

The Union in Peril, Lincoln Calls

THE YEARS ROLLED BY ON the Illinois prairie. Many more settlers joined the Brown family in Mercer County. What was once wild land was tamed by the horse-drawn plow and the toil of pioneer families. Gone were the days of the log cabin, but perilous times approached like a towering thunderhead on the prairie horizon. The Whig Party, which had been one of the two major political parties in the United States since the time the Browns arrived in Illinois until the early 1850s, met its end. The party collapsed when the Kansas-Nebraska Act passed Congress in 1854. The Act overturned the Missouri Compromise and its use of latitude (36 degrees, 30 minutes north parallel) as the boundary between slave and free territory. Under the Act, which also created the territories of Nebraska and Kansas, settlers of a new territory were authorized to decide whether to allow or prohibit slavery by "popular sovereignty." This set off intensified conflict between pro-slavery and anti-slavery settlers, a prelude to an even deeper divide ahead. Most Northern Whigs, like Abraham Lincoln and Joshua's father, Benjamin Franklin Brown, joined the new anti-slavery Republican Party. In fact, Mercer County played an early role in the party's creation. In the summer of 1854, meetings were called in at least two townships in the county and resolutions were adopted calling for the formation of a new political party to oppose the expansion of slavery under the Kansas-Nebraska Act.[16]

Astonishingly, although it had just been formed, the Republican Party gained control of the U.S. House of Representatives by 1855. Benjamin became a "zealous and active adherent,"[17] which undoubtedly shaped Joshua's political views. Benjamin's brother (Joshua's uncle), Samuel W. Brown, was elected to the Illinois legislature in 1854, where he supported Abe Lincoln in his bid that year for a seat in the United States Senate (Senators were selected in those days by state legislatures).[18] Lincoln lost his bid for the office, but Samuel and Lincoln would become close personal friends.[19]

Despite the political turmoil, these were good years for the Browns. Benjamin continued building the family farm, acquiring 324 acres "upon which he prospered to the extent that eventually he built an extremely fine residence in 1861."[20] As a growing state, Illinois was feeling its new influence. Just five years after losing his initial bid for the Senate, Illinois's own Abraham Lincoln had been elected President of the United States in November 1860. Things took an ominous turn, however, on April 12th, 1861, when shots were fired half a continent away at Fort Sumter, South Carolina.

At first, even the advent of war between the states did not change life much in what was still a rural and isolated part of the country. That was about to change—and how.

The Formation of the 84th Illinois Infantry Volunteers

"The Spring and Summer of 1862 were fraught with stirring events. The war had been in progress a year, vast armies had been sent into the field, but as yet only a small portion of the Confederate States had been passed over by our forces."[21] Things were not going well for the Union. "The army of the Mississippi had hardly advanced to the northern boundary of Mississippi and Alabama: the army of the Potomac was toiling upon the Peninsula, and at every point our troops were met by equal and at many points by superior numbers."[22]

President Abraham Lincoln

President Lincoln feared that further signs of weakness could prompt European powers to enter the fray on the side of the Confederacy, turning the tide of the war. The future of the United States was on the line. To meet the challenge, Lincoln needed more soldiers. "It was evident to all thinking minds, that more troops must be speedily sent to the scenes of action, or the suppression of the great rebellion would indeed prove a failure."[23] So, President Lincoln took decisive action. "The President [on] about the 1st of June 1862, issued his proclamation calling for fifty thousand more volunteers to serve for the term of three years, or during the war."[24]

Between June and August of 1862, public meetings to recruit volunteers were held across Illinois, including in Mercer County. However, during this time, the situation worsened, and even more volunteers were needed. "[T]he army of the Potomac had met with terrible reverses: the Army in Southern Tennessee was being forced back into Kentucky: the President in this emergency had called for three hundred thousand volunteers: and the quota for Illinois now being about forty regiments instead of four."[25] The dire nature of the situation was not lost on the loyal Illinois populace. They responded in large numbers—and at great personal sacrifice. "Now it was, that the peril of our government became apparent to every one: farmers left their crops standing in the field and mechanics threw aside their tools. "[26] During July and early August of 1862 ten companies were organized for the 84th Infantry Regiment of Illinois Volunteers.

One of the first volunteers who answered the call at this critical time to help preserve the Union was Joshua Hobbs Brown. Joshua was still a young man. It was only 16 days past his 21st birthday, on July 22nd, 1862, when he enlisted as a Private in the newly forming Company H which was comprised of volunteers from Mercer County. Enlistment records show Joshua's home as North Henderson, in the southeast corner of the county. This, of course, was the family farm in North Henderson Township. Also enlisting in Company H on the same day was John Webster Dilley, Joshua's future brother-in-law. In just three weeks, they would leave their families and the familiar Illinois prairie for an unknown future.

The official organization of Company H was completed at Keithsburg, Illinois on August 14th.[27] After saying his goodbyes to his mom, dad, and siblings, the young man with the wavy brown hair from North Henderson joined the other men of Company H on their way to war. They boarded a steamboat and headed down the mighty Mississippi bound for Quincy, Illinois, more than 120 miles to the south. They arrived on the 15th.[28] The volunteers then began vigorous drills as well as studying military regulations and tactics.[29] "By the end of the month we were said to be ready for muster into the U.S. service, awaited somewhat anxiously the arrival of the mustering officer, to make us part of the grand army of the Union."[30] Joshua and his Company were formally mustered into service on September 1st, 1862, at Quincy. The original "muster in" rolls show that Company H consisted of 95 enlisted men and three officers.[31] Fewer than five score in number, they were destined for peril and heartache beyond their deepest fears and glory beyond their youthful hopes.

Before long, it was time to say farewell to their loved ones. No one knew when they would see home again. Many would not. On September 4th, a "large picnic party" from neighboring towns visited the Regiment's camp to see them off. It was an emotional time for the young volunteers. "[W]hen the hour for separation and parting came, pearly tears were welling from more eyes than belonged to fond mothers, wives, daughters, and sweethearts."[32]

The troops would not depart to confront the enemy in the South, though, for nearly three weeks. In the meantime, more drilling and preparation was in store. On September 14th, the Regiment was armed with long Enfield rifle muskets. This English-made musket weighed nine and a half pounds and was 55 inches long. Depending on conditions and the skill of the user, it could fire about five rounds a minute. Joshua was also provided a knapsack, haversack, and canteen. He was now fully prepared for active duty.[33]

CHAPTER THREE

Red Trail in the Snow

IN THE LATTER HALF OF 1862, Confederate General Braxton Bragg led an invasion by Rebel forces into Kentucky. He sought to bring that state into the Confederacy, gather supplies and recruit new troops.[34] Faced with losing territory, the Union needed to respond. The force assigned to protect Kentucky from the Confederates' advance was the Army of the Ohio led by Union General Don Buell. Joshua and the new 84th Illinois Infantry Regiment would soon join them in this effort. The "Kentucky campaign," as it was called, would be Joshua's first experience with war. It would start with modest success on the battlefield but end with a ghastly trail of suffering stained with his own Regiment's blood.

The Kentucky Campaign

The Kentucky campaign was largely a disaster for the Union. It was destined to be costly and brutal, but not on the battlefield. Poor planning, lack of supplies and bad weather nearly destroyed the 84th Illinois Regiment. How Joshua survived can only be described as a wonder.

Imagine a 21-year-old farm boy stepping off a troop train on his first day in the war theater and being faced with the *immediate* prospect of a full-scale battle to control an important city. This was the hair-raising beginning of the Kentucky campaign for Joshua.[35] On September 23rd, 1862, Joshua and his Regiment were loaded on train cars in Quincy, Illinois, bound for the "Gateway to the South," Louisville, Kentucky.[36] When they arrived on the 26th they were surprised to see the city in a state of alarm. Attack from the Confederate Army was considered imminent. "We had scarcely laid off camp when the regiment was ordered to move. Lines of battle were hastily formed in the street and an attack was during the whole night momentarily expected." But the attack never came. The newly reinforced Union Army dissuaded General Bragg from attempting to take Louisville. The Confederates were now falling back, and on October 1st, the whole Union Army that was encamped at Louisville started out in pursuit of Bragg's Confederate troops who were retreating towards Danville, Kentucky.[37]

The Battle of Perryville

While battle did not come for Joshua that first day at Louisville, it was soon to follow. Bragg now halted his retreat and went on the attack. On October 8th, near the town of Perryville, Kentucky, groups of soldiers from both armies began skirmishing for control of the only water source in the area. Intense fighting followed. It went back and forth with no clear overall advantage. Joshua's Regiment was engaged in the battle but was not at the center of the fighting. Hostilities ceased when darkness set in, but all knew it was to resume in the morning. Twenty-two thousand Union soldiers formed a line in the Chaplin Hills west of Perryville during the night. Sixteen thousand Confederates lined up on the east side of the river. Bragg, who wrongly believed he was facing only part of the Union forces, planned a full attack. During the night, however, Bragg discovered he was actually facing the entire Army of the Ohio. He decided to pull back and head toward Tennessee taking large amounts of captured supplies. To the dismay of national leaders in Washington, General Buell did not pursue.

The stalemate at Perryville was the high point of the Kentucky campaign for the Union and for Joshua's Regiment. What followed is hard to imagine today. Hunger, exposure, bitter cold, and disease pursued the Union troops. For many of them, it was the end of the story. For Joshua and the 84th Illinois, their service nearly ended less than a month after it began.

Red Trail in the Snow

Within a week after Perryville, supplies began to run low and hunger stalked Joshua's Regiment. A member of the Regiment, who would become its chief historian, wrote that on October 17th, 1862, "We now began really to suffer from scant rations, and for the ensuing twenty days this was the constant complaint."[38] On the 19th, Joshua's supper was a small ration of poor beef with salt—not even a cracker or a cup of coffee.[39] The next day, on an empty stomach, Joshua and his Regiment were ordered to march 32 miles without "a particle of food or a cup of coffee."[40] That was not the worst of what was to come—not even close.

The tragic scene was set on October 23rd: "From Mt. Vernon [Kentucky] we took the road to Somerset and encamped the first night at Buck Creek. Early in the evening a cold, chilly rain set in, and we made the best shelter we could of brush and our single blankets and built large fires."[41] Things then took a turn for the worse. "Before 10 o'clock a snow storm set in, and by daylight, at least a foot of snow had fallen."[42] This freak October snowstorm would be bad news for any army; but for the 84th Infantry it was deadly. The tragedy that followed was compounded by misfortune. "Our men were scantily clothed, for the weather had been very warm for a few days after leaving Louisville."[43] Being overloaded, "they had thrown away all except one suit and many now were nearly bare footed and some had been so unfortunate as to lose, or have their blankets stolen by the older regiments of the Brigade."[44] The 84th was the only new regiment assigned to the Brigade and was on the receiving end of much "mirth and ridicule" and, more ominously, theft of supplies by senior regiments.

What occurred next that morning in late October of 1862 near Somerset, Kentucky was difficult to adequately describe even by those who experienced it firsthand. "[T]his terrible morning, and the tedious march that day in snow, water, slush and mud to Somerset—we must despair of fairly portraying its hardships." The march out of the snow-covered encampment "dragged on for twelve tedious miles."[45]

The blunt truth is that Joshua's 84th Illinois Regiment literally left a trail of blood in the snow as they marched those fateful, freezing miles. The Report of the Adjutant General of the State of Illinois stated that "In the march from Buck Creek to Somerset, a distance of 12 miles, some 90 of the men were compelled to wade through snow, slush and mud the entire distance without shoes."[46]

Eyewitnesses reported that "while bringing in cedar boughs to build a shelter in the night, we noticed, as we had frequently during the day dry blood stained foot prints in the snow—blood from the sore and lacerated and almost frozen feet of the soldiers." The next day scores of the men "were sent out to the Hospital, some never to return again."[47] Joshua, being young and resilient from pioneer living, somehow survived.

After recovering a spell, Joshua and those of his Company H who were able, marched onward in pursuit of the Confederates and General Bragg. On November 10th, 1862, they crossed the state line from Kentucky into Tennessee.[48]

By mid-November, Union General Buell, "having made a complete failure of the Kentucky campaign,"[49] was replaced by General William Rosecrans. Under this new command, the Army of the Ohio became known as the Army of the Cumberland. The new leadership was "received with shouts of joy" as Buell had become "despised" by the troops. [50] Rosecrans reorganized the army and the 84th Illinois was placed in the 3rd Brigade under the command of Colonel William Gross. The 3rd Brigade was part of the 2nd Division (under General Souey Smith) of the 21st Army Corps under Major General Crittenden.[51]

Exposure, rain, snow, sickness, and the rigors of long marches and camp life with scant rations took their toll. By the time Joshua and his Regiment reached winter quarters near Nashville, only about 400 men were fit for duty out of more than 900 who had left Illinois.[52] The Kentucky campaign had produced little gain militarily, and it cost the Regiment more men than any single battle to come. The sacrifices borne by those who left their homes and families on the Illinois prairie at Lincoln's call to save the Union were many. And as the hardships of the Kentucky campaign showed, these sacrifices included far more than even the horrific struggles on battlefields to come.

If we suppose that American slavery is one of those offenses which in the providence of God . . . He now wills to remove and that He gives to both North and South this terrible war as the woe due to those by whom the offense came. . . . Fondly do we hope—fervently do we pray—that this mighty scourge of war may speedily pass away. Yet, if God wills that it continue until all the wealth piled by the bondsman's two hundred and fifty years of unrequited toil shall be sunk and until every drop of blood drawn with the lash shall be paid by another drop of blood drawn with the sword . . . it must be said "the judgments of the Lord are true and righteous altogether." [53] Abraham Lincoln

CHAPTER FOUR

Emancipation Vindication

The Battle of Stones River

IN 1860, NEARLY FOUR MILLION human beings in the United States—one out of eight people—were enslaved. The emancipation of these slaves, after years of intense national debate as well as fervent prayer and sustained pressure from abolitionists, was initiated by the courage, strategy, and political will of President Abraham Lincoln. However, proclaiming freedom and making it a reality are two different things. Freeing these oppressed millions from chains and shackles, forced labor and loss of human dignity, as well as from brutal whippings and rape at the hands of slave masters across the South, was proclaimed on paper, but it was accomplished on the battlefield.

The Civil War had been raging for well over a year, and by late 1862 the Union Army had lost its momentum against the Confederacy. President Lincoln was in desperate need of a victory. Success was especially critical as the calendar approached the new year since Lincoln's Emancipation Proclamation freeing the slaves in the South was set to take effect on January 1st, 1863. If the situation on the battlefield did not back up his bold move to free the slaves, the Emancipation Proclamation would likely be perceived as a hollow gesture. The future of the United States and the freedom of millions of enslaved men, women and children was at stake.

Just two months after Perryville, the 84th Illinois Regiment would face its first big test on the battlefield, and one of its deadliest. Joshua's Regiment had been at winter camp near Nashville since November 26th. The day after Christmas they moved out towards Murfreesboro in pursuit of the Confederate Army.[54] The Regiment was still feeling the severe effects of the Kentucky campaign and that deadly snowstorm near Somerset. "When we started on the march from Nashville toward Murfreesboro, there were of the whole Regiment fit for duty, only twenty-five officers and three hundred thirty-seven enlisted men, the remainder being in convalescent camps and hospitals."[55]

Union forces were under the command of Major General William Rosecrans. He had been based at Nashville after Confederate General Braxton Bragg and the Army of the Tennessee exited Kentucky following their retreat from Perryville.[56] Rosecrans had divided his army into three wings. These were under Major Generals McCook, Thomas, and Crittendon, respectively.[57]

On December 29th Joshua's Regiment neared Murfreesboro. As they marched that day, the 84th, along with the 36th Indiana and the 23rd Kentucky, were in the "front line of battle" position.[58] By dusk, they were two miles from Murfreesboro and just a mile from Stones River.[59]

So, at this momentous time in American history, the Army of the Cumberland (which included the 84th Illinois Infantry) and the Confederate Army of Tennessee were preparing to engage at Stones River near Murfreesboro, Tennessee. The number of soldiers involved was considerable. Over 80,000 men massed for the confrontation. This was Joshua's first major battle, and it would last from December 30th, 1862 to January 2nd, 1863—precisely at the time the Emancipation Proclamation was to take effect. The Battle of Stones River (or Battle of Murfreesboro, as it was known in the South) would prove to be one of the bloodiest battles of the entire Civil War.

On December 30th, skirmishing between the opposing forces was constant. What were then known as "sharpshooters" harassed the 84th's front line from hidden Confederate positions along the railroad line leading into Murfreesboro. "Many a [musket] ball during the day whistled through the lines of the 84th."[60] This was just a prelude to what was coming. The men of the 84th "knew a great battle was about to be fought, and the boys were anxious for the ball to open."[61]

Accounts of the battle are as chilling as they are moving. On December 30th, 1862, the "fighting died down by sunset and more than 81,000 soldiers turned their attention toward preparing for the carnage that was sure to come the next day. Generals Bragg and Rosecrans assessed their positions and prepared their attack plans. As the sun sank below the horizon, temperatures plummeted below freezing."[62] As if the cold was not bad enough, precipitation began to fall. "Darkness enveloped the landscape. Cold rain showers pelted [the] miserable soldiers. The men did what they could to stay warm and dry."[63] More discomforting than the rain, though, was the prospect of what lay ahead. "Some sat silently contemplating the coming fight. Most thought of their homes and families, and many wrote letters to their loved ones by candlelight knowing those words might be the last they ever wrote. In many places the opposing armies were separated by only a few hundred yards."[64]

If this scene was not remarkable enough, something utterly amazing was about to take place.

Home Sweet Home

One of the overriding aspects of the War Against the Rebellion, of course, is that it was a civil war—a war between two opposing camps of one people. They shared one nation, one common language, predominantly one religion and one common national heritage. They were in many ways one family in the middle of a tragic and deadly fight. All had dreams of making it back home alive. As it happened, both sides had military bands in their camps that night to boost the morale of the soldiers. Seldom in history has something so moving occurred on a battlefield.

> The bands of both sides began playing to cheer the men. The strains of "Dixie" and "Yankee Doodle," and other patriotic airs echoed through the darkness. . . .
>
> [W]hat happened next . . . proved to be one of the most poignant moments on any battlefield: Finally, one of them struck up 'Home, Sweet Home.' As if by common consent all other airs ceased, and the bands of both armies, far as the ear could reach, joined in the refrain.
>
> Some men lifted their voices to join the now united bands. Others put their faces into their hats lest their comrades spy their tears. Certainly, every man's thoughts turned toward home and the bitter prospect that many would never live to see it.[65]

One wonders what mixed memories of cherished comradery and dreadful loss filled Joshua's mind in later years when he again heard that song.

Joshua is Wounded, Emancipation is Vindicated and the 84th Illinois Volunteers Earn Their Reputation for Valiant Combat

The next day the carnage was indeed massive. It was New Year's Eve, 1862. Things did not start or end well for the Union. "At daylight the battle commenced on the extreme right of the army and [from the perspective of the Illinois 84th] gradually drew nearer. . . . It was now evident the whole army had been flanked during the night."[66] The Union Army's lines were being folded like a jackknife by the Confederate's early morning attack. The next thing young Joshua would observe was like a scene from a horror novel.

> Now out of the thick cedars came a host of fugitives from the broken Corps on our right. Terrible sight! Hundreds, yes thousands of men, many of whom had thrown away guns, cartridge boxes and knapsacks, each looking as though death was at each moment expected, terror the

17

only expression upon their countenances, as through our lines they came, on a run or brisk walk, panting, from fear and fatigue, and they could not be rallied.[67]

The battle was nearing a tipping point. The Union forces continued to be pushed back toward the rail line and the Pike (the road leading through Murfreesboro), and the advancing Rebels were getting closer to the position of the 84th. "Soon the heavy firing told that the enemy were sweeping all before them, and coming directly upon us, from our new front and right."[68] For the men of the 84th it was like standing in the path of an oncoming tidal wave. "Each moment the crowd of stragglers increased in number, each moment the firing became more rapid and nearer to us."[69]

Joshua and his Regiment, however, did not panic or retreat. With courage summoned from somewhere deep within they held their position and their ground. By doing so, they helped preserve the Emancipation Proclamation that was set to take effect at midnight.

"Soon the enemy came out of the woods about three or four hundred yards in our front. Our boys sprang up with a loud shout and gave them a volley, then laid down and loaded and fired at will."[70] The Confederates were driven back into the woods. But the battle was far from over. "Our Regiment was now terribly exposed . . . for the enemy were coming in upon us through thick cedars."[71] After enduring withering fire for another hour the enemy was now within 60 yards of the 84th. The situation was dire. The Regiment "fought desperately, every man working as though his life depended upon his own exertions."[72] The 84th sought refuge near a low ridge of rocks west of the Pike and fought for another hour.[73] But things did not improve. "The enemy was pouring upon us a most galling fire as we lay in this position, the balls falling like hail in a heavy storm."[74] The 84th was ordered to fall back and things did not look good for the Union or Lincoln's Emancipation Proclamation.

As the 84th fell back, Union artillery was let loose on the pursuing but now-exposed Confederate troops. The barrage from the battery allowed what was left of the 84th to escape. Joshua's Regiment, however, had borne a terrible toll. While positioned along the ledge of rock near the Pike and while falling back to the railroad, "twenty-five of the Regiment fell dead, and scores were wounded."[75] Many were from Joshua's Company H.

The "Slaughter Pen" at Stones River National Battlefield.

The battle had been intense and prolonged. For hour after hour of pure hell the 84th had fought on. "We had been in the heat of the engagement for six terrible hours, and the Regiment was more than decimated."[76] But their effort made an important difference. "The very decisive stand made by our Brigade and Division seems to have turned the tide of battle."[77] They had kept the Confederates from completely overtaking the Union lines and ending the battle. The 84th Illinois paid a heavy price for this valiant stand. "Tears flowed down the cheeks of our brave colonel when he counted only 113 guns in the stacks" that evening.[78] "Each survivor had lost comrades and friends, and several found near and dear kinsmen and brothers missing."[79]

Having inflicted such severe casualties on the North, and having pushed them back to the rail line, Bragg expected the beleaguered Union forces would retreat during the night. He was wrong. When New Year's Day dawned, the boys in blue were still there holding their line.

For the remainder of January 1st both armies largely ceased fighting in order to regroup. The second day of January, however, brought an encore of the fierce battle. Despite having been pushed back to the rail line, the Union still held some high ground on the north side of the river, and Bragg ordered his troops to attack it. Union General Van Cleve's Division was

19

attacked by five Brigades of Confederate infantry and it was being routed—so much so that at this point the Confederates thought they had won. "The whole [Union] division was in full retreat. . . . Out of the woods, pursuing them came the Brigades of the enemy . . . apparently secure of an early and complete victory."[80]

What the Rebels did not know, and could not anticipate, was that the 84th was waiting for them and would not join the retreat. Before combat had commenced that day, the Regiment constructed a breastwork of logs so as to have at least some modest protection. The Illinois 84th was lying in wait behind it. More importantly, perhaps, General Rosecrans had prepared a deadly surprise for the Confederates. "Soon the several batteries massed by order of General Rosecrans on the opposite bank of the river began to pour a heavy fire into the enemy."[81] At about this time, "the 84th Illinois and Sixth Ohio raised with a yell and gave them a volley, then loaded and fired at will."[82] What followed is a page out of history. "The 84th Illinois and Sixth Ohio now sprang over their breastworks with a yell that was heard three miles and charged the enemy, who were soon in full retreat."[83] The 84th pursued the fleeing Rebels for half a mile, but since they were running low on ammunition, the 84th returned to their breastworks for the night. The 84th lost one man and three others were severely wounded, but their spirits were greatly revived. "[T]he reverse of Wednesday [the 31st] was scarcely remembered in view of the brilliant success of to-day, which had virtually decided the battle of Stones River."[84]

The human toll that day was unimaginable. The 84th had the gruesome task of surveying the aftermath. "The loss of the enemy in the open field and woods was immense. We were over the field in the evening and the dead were lying in heaps, and hundreds [of] wounded were on every side."[85]

Total Union casualties reached 1,677 killed and 7,543 wounded. Confederate casualties were 1,294 killed and 7,945 wounded. Altogether, more than 3,000 Americans lost their lives and more than 18,000 were wounded. "Of all the major battles of the American Civil War, the Battle of Stones River had the highest percentage of casualties."[86] The casualty rate exceeded 29%. One eyewitness summarized the feeling of all: "The immense slaughter of our brave men chills and sickens us all."[87]

Young Joshua Brown was among those badly wounded at Stones River.[88] The precise details are lost to history. What we do know is that his wounds were severe. We also know his injury was from a gunshot (and not a bayonet or other cause). Finally, we know he never left his Regiment. The latter fact would indicate he may have been shot towards the end of the battle since a severely wounded soldier would likely have become separated from the Regiment over time. Joshua lost many friends. His Company H lost nine men, including three from John Webster Dilley's hometown of Ohio Grove. Joshua's Company H lost both its 1st Lieutenant and 2nd Lieutenant on the battlefield.[89] In all, 33 three men from his Regiment were killed in battle. One hundred fourteen were severely wounded, of whom 31 later died of their wounds.[90] To put this in context, remember that because of the heavy loss of men during the Kentucky campaign, only 350 from the Regiment were engaged.[91] "In proportion to the number of men, [the 84th] probably lost more heavily than any Regiment in the Division, and perhaps in the army."[92]

This great sacrifice and the valor that preceded it would earn the 84th its heroic reputation. They laid down their lives for their country, for freedom, and their brothers- in-arms. As scripture says, "Greater love has no man than this: to lay down one's life for one's friends."[93] The 84th Infantry Regiment "by valiant service on this memorable occasion secured a glorious reputation."[94] A history written in 1885 stated, "One of the most gallant regiments of a gallant state was the one known as the 84th infantry."[95]

By January 4th, the Confederate Army had withdrawn, and the Union forces entered Murfreesboro around 4:00 p.m.[96] The result of the Battle of Stones River was a hard-fought and important victory for the Union. The *New York Times* reported, "The New Year of 1863 will long be remembered for the blows that were struck and blood which flowed on the ground of Murfreesboro. . . . The battle of Murfreesboro or Stones River, is the most remarkable of the war."[97]

The Battle of Stones River was most significant for its impact on the Emancipation Proclamation and its positive momentum for the Union. "[D]efeat would have made the Emancipation Proclamation look like the last gasp of a dying war effort and perhaps brought England and France into the war on the side of the Confederacy."[98] Instead, with the victory Union troops became liberators. Enslaved Blacks began to flee in larger numbers, seeking safety in the shelter of Northern armies. Public opinion also shifted in favor of Lincoln's efforts at a time when support for the war had been wavering. President Lincoln considered the victory so important that "the nation could scarcely have lived" if there "had been a defeat instead."[99]

For the mothers, fathers, siblings, and grandparents back home in Mercer County, the Battle of Stones River brought a time of great apprehension and, for far too many, their worst nightmares. Lengthy, detailed descriptions of eye-witness accounts of the battle appeared in the *Aledo (Illinois) Weekly Record*. However, they were not printed until January 13th. Appropriately, these accounts appeared on page one right next to the announcement of "The Proclamation" of the President of the United States of America—the Emancipation Proclamation. A field report dated January 1st, 1863, with a dateline of Nashville stated, "I have just arrived from a terrific battle on Stones River. . . . It has raged with unremitting fury for two days. . . . It is one of the most ferocious battles of modern times."[100] Another report in the same paper with a Nashville dateline of January 2nd noted, "The terrible battle of Stones River is not yet decided." The story went on to paint a bleak picture of the Union's chances. "[W]hen the battle closed the enemy occupied the ground which was ours in the morning, and the advantage is, therefore, in their favor."[101] It also reported that "The cannonading was heard at Nashville." When one realizes this is a distance of over 30 miles, the intensity of the battle comes into focus.

Ominously, the reporter noted, "Great numbers of wounded are being brought in now." One can imagine the deep anguish of the many family members of the Illinois 84th as they read these words back in Mercer County, not knowing the fate of their loved ones. A week later, the *Aledo Weekly Record* reported the dreadful number of casualties. What is especially heart rending, is that the story featured not the 84th Illinois Infantry Regiment as a whole, but rather Joshua's Company H (referred to locally as Captain Pepper's Company). "A feeling of sadness was manifest throughout our entire community, on receipt of the list of killed and wounded in Cap't Peppers' Co. 84th Regiment last week. This Company was the first one raised in the County under the last calls of the President and we believe this was the first battle in which they have been engaged."[102] The headline read "Our Losses at Murfreesboro" and the piercing sub-headline read, "Nine killed, Eighteen Wounded, And Two Missing in Capt. Pepper's Co." It must be repeated, this was just the toll from Joshua's Company H, which even at its beginning had fewer than one hundred men. The paper also reported "The total number of killed, wounded and missing in the 84th is as follows: 37 killed, 18 wounded, and 4 missing." This preliminary casualty report would grow as more men died from their wounds. The loss at Stones River to the little farming communities in Mercer County was staggering.

Today at the Stones River National Battlefield in Murfreesboro, not far from Nashville, visitors can walk in the former cottonfield where Joshua's Company H was positioned and where Joshua was wounded during the battle, examine cannons like the ones that set the stage for the Union victory, and view the rows upon rows of marble grave stones marking the resting places of the 1,677 Union soldiers, including many from little Mercer County, Illinois, who gave their lives that day.

Union cannon at Stones River National Battlefield Cemetery.
Photo by Steve Grasz

Stones River National Battlefield Cemetery.
Photo by Steve Grasz

Stones River was Joshua's first major battle, but it would by no means be his last. Although seriously wounded, he never left his regiment for even a day—a fact his granddaughter would proudly recount to Joshua's great-great grandchildren a century later.[103] Amazingly, Joshua went on to fight in many other of the most famous battles of the Civil War including the Battles of Chickamauga, Atlanta, Nashville, Franklin, Lookout Mountain, Missionary Ridge, and Kennesaw Mountain. He was also in a number of other battles such as Ringold, Resaca, Jonesboro, Buzzard's Roost Gap, Dallas, Peachtree Creek, and Lovejoy Station besides many skirmishes with the Confederates along the way.

CHAPTER FIVE

Defeat at the River of Death

The Tullahoma Campaign and the Capture of Chattanooga

FOLLOWING THE BATTLE OF STONES River both armies remained in Central Tennessee for months to regroup and recover from the battle. This was no small task. "The condition of the wounded during this great battle was deplorable."[104] With so many casualties, the army field hospitals were unable to procure enough tents for about a tenth of the wounded. "Nearly all for two or three days had to lie out of doors, upon the damp ground, covered only with blankets, and having a good fire at their feet."[105] Keep in mind this was in January. The medical response was primitive but massive. "Here were acres of ground covered with hospital tents, all of which were full of wounded men, nearly 4,000 in all, and wounded in every possible manner."[106]

With the area firmly in Union control, General Rosecrans and his Army of the Cumberland proceeded to construct a large Union base at Murfreesboro. Confederate General Bragg took defensive positions further south near Tullahoma to guard approaches the Union might take to the key railroad town of Chattanooga near the Tennessee-Georgia border.[107] In June, however, Rosecrans surprised Bragg with an advance. Bragg was forced to pull back to the Tennessee River and Chattanooga. The Union Army pursued.

Joshua and his 84th Illinois Regiment began their advance toward Chattanooga on August 16th, 1863.[108] They marched their way down the Sequatchee Valley to the Tennessee River past Jasper. The Tennessee

River was a major riverboat highway and by no means an easy crossing. On September 3rd, the Regiment built rafts on which to cross the imposing river. However, many of the men placed their knapsacks and guns on the rafts and swam across.[109] Since he grew up not far from the Mississippi River, one can imagine Joshua joined them. By September 7th, the 84th neared Chattanooga, which was still in possession of the Rebels. Joshua and his Company could see the enemy's signal stations on Lookout Mountain.[110] On the 9th, Joshua beheld a vista that made quite an impression on the Regiment:

> The prospect that met our view when we reached Summerville was grand beyond description. We were upon a high bluff, nearly two thousand feet above the Tennessee River. The city of Chattanooga, now nearly deserted, was only about two miles and a half distant and so much beneath that we could look down into all its streets. Long lines of dust marked the road, upon which the enemy were retreating.[111]

The Union Army was elated at the sight. "Chattanooga, the key to East Tennessee, one of the great railroad centers and military depots of the Confederacy, was in our possession, without a battle."[112]

Yes, Rosecrans had again outmaneuvered Bragg, and the Confederates had abandoned Chattanooga without a fight, to regroup in North Georgia. "The Tullahoma Campaign ended in the capture of Chattanooga and the remainder of middle Tennessee for much of the rest of the war at a cost of only 560 casualties."[113] However, "Rosecrans' overconfidence resulting from the ease of the capture of Chattanooga would lead him to divide his army and risk destruction at the battle of Chickamauga."[114]

The Battle of Chickamauga

The easy capture of Chattanooga was encouraging to the men. However, everyone knew that a "momentous conflict was about to take place."[115] After pushing Braxton Bragg's Army of Tennessee out of Chattanooga, General Rosecrans gathered his army of 60,000 men twelve miles to the southeast at Chickamauga, Georgia. Perhaps the Union troops had no idea that "Chickamauga" means "river of death." Certainly, they did not know their good fortunes were about to be reversed. The Confederates were not retreating in disorder, as Rosecrans thought, and his decision to split his army into three corps to pursue them turned out to be a tragic error. "Ere the sun went down, on the evening of the 17th of September, every soldier in the whole army felt that the battle must within a few hours commence."[116] As they had the night before the battle at Stones River, the men of Joshua's Regiment thought of home. "Many while resting would pencil a few hasty lines to the loved ones at home, and many would take from their knapsacks and cartridge boxes, their last letters received from dear and cherished sweethearts, wives and mothers."[117] And, as at Stones River, the next day did bring carnage and death.

"From two o'clock until the sun went down, a ball of fire as seen through the smoke of the battlefield, this terrible conflict raged with unabated fury.[118] The fortunes of the two great armies ebbed and flowed. "At times our forces would be driven back by the desperate charges and overwhelming numbers which opposed them; then they would rally, and with a yell, charge and scatter the rebels, and drive them far back into the dense forest."[119] When it was over, Joshua was still standing and not seriously wounded. Many others were not so fortunate. Eleven men in his Regiment were killed. Seventy-seven others were severely wounded and 12 more were missing.[120] "[M]any of our bravest men had gone down amid the furious din of battle, and breathed out their noble lives upon the bloody field, while the leaden rain and iron hail was sweeping down the hosts that were charging over them."[121]

Given the ferocity of the battle, the 84th Illinois fared relatively well. Overall, the Battle of Chickamauga produced the second-highest number of casualties of the Civil War after Gettysburg. The Union lost 1,657 killed and 9,756 wounded. The Confederacy had 2,312 killed and 14,674 wounded. Including those captured or missing on both sides, casualties totaled 34,624 out of approximately 125,000 combatants, "making the Battle of Chickamauga the costliest one in the war's western theater."[122]

The result was a victory for the Confederacy. The Army of the Cumberland, after being overwhelmed by the superior Confederate force at Chickamauga, retreated to a line of defense in front of Chattanooga.[123]

CHAPTER SIX

The Chattanooga Campaign

Under Siege

WHEN THE HARDSHIPS OF WAR come to mind, they are usually connected to fierce combat. However, in the case of the Civil War, they also frequently included less dramatic but often just as deadly perils such as disease, hunger, and grueling physical exertion and stress. Joshua faced all of these.

Having retreated to the outskirts of Chattanooga after the defeat at Chickamauga to defend the strategic railroad junction, Joshua and the 84th Regiment set to work building fortified lines. "For more than a week after taking these positions, our army was almost incessantly employed in the throwing up a strong line of fortifications. Night and day the work went on."[124] The fortifications were not without good cause. Bragg's Army of Tennessee surrounded the city to the south, taking positions on Lookout Mountain and Missionary Ridge to cut off supply routes to the Union forces. The city and the Union forces were now under siege.

Less than a month after the Battle of Chickamauga, Joshua and his Regiment began to face the prospect of starvation. "As early as the 14th of October, the whole force hemmed in at Chattanooga were reduced to an allowance of less than half rations of pork, hard tack, sugar and coffee, and these were the only articles of diet that could be furnished."[125] And it got worse from there. "By the 20th, rations were still more pinched and scanty."[126]

In response, President Lincoln ordered Major General Ulysses S. Grant to Chattanooga. Grant quickly implemented a daring plan to open a supply line and begin offensive maneuvers to lift the siege. To bolster the Union forces, Grant moved Sherman's Army of the Tennessee to the city.[127] Joshua and his comrades were elated. "This was hailed with shouts and cheers, long, loud and jubilant."[128] Rather than await starvation, Grant wanted to change the status quo. By the third week of November 1863, the besieged troops were prepared to go on the offensive.

Battle Above the Clouds and the Charge Up Missionary Ridge

What followed is part of Civil War lore and yet another reason why the 84th Illinois Infantry Regiment achieved such acclaim. Having gained battlefield glory at Stones River and shocking defeat at Chickamauga, the Illinois 84th was not content to let the Confederacy's newly regained momentum last. Overlooking Chattanooga, Tennessee was the strategically important high ground of Lookout Mountain. Rising to 2,392 feet above sea level, the mountain provided views of any troop movements in the area. Seven states are said to be visible from the summit. It also provided key positions for Confederate artillery. The summit of the mountain lies in Georgia while its southwest section is in Alabama. To end the siege of Chattanooga and open supply routes, the Confederate positions on both Lookout Mountain and Missionary Ridge had to be taken. Taking Lookout Mountain would be an improbable and spectacular accomplishment. The mountain was securely in the hands of the enemy and a direct assault on its steep slopes seemed impossible. "[U]p to this time the rank and file of the army, at least in our Division, had scarcely imagined that General Hooker would attempt to take Lookout Mountain, itself almost inaccessible, and now strongly fortified, by storm."[129] And yet, take it by storm they did.

On November 24th, the peak of Lookout Mountain was shrouded in clouds. Some would say it was a scene made for cinema. Others would say it was evidence of God's providential hand. The fighting that followed would become known as the "Battle Above the Clouds." Under cover of the clouds and fog covering the peak of Lookout Mountain, Joshua's Regiment amazingly managed to advance up the steep mountain slopes undetected. The Union troops climbed up and up its steep sides until they appeared near the summit. The surprised Confederate defenders were soon overpowered. By the next morning, "just as the sun was rising, the Star Spangled Banner floated out proudly to the breeze, from the towering summit of Lookout Mountain."[130]

This feat would have been magnificent by itself. But God's providence was not spent. A second miracle followed the next day. Missionary Ridge surrounds what is today downtown Chattanooga. It has steep vertical sides that rise well over 300 feet from its base. Like Lookout Mountain, its capture was essential to opening supply routes to the besieged Union troops. On the 25th, the Army of the Cumberland was ordered to attack the Confederate rifle pits at the base of Missionary Ridge and then regroup. The pits were readily captured, but the Union forces were then easily fired upon from above. Another cinematic scene followed. "In one of the most dramatic moments of the war, the Army of the Cumberland, without clear and specific orders to do so, charged up Missionary Ridge."[131] Yes, they courageously launched a direct assault up the steep fortified ridge. "Up they went, without firing a shot, over rocks, trees, and stumps, surmounted the crest, captured the guns and turned them upon the enemy, now fully routed, and in disorderly retreat."[132]

Assaulting two fortified summits in two days by climbing up the steep slopes to vanquish a well-armed enemy is astonishing. But keep in mind that Joshua's Regiment had been under siege, with supply lines cut, for 40 days. He and his comrades had been surviving on little food and were malnourished. Some developed scurvy, including Joshua's fellow Company H soldier and future brother-in-law, John Webster Dilley.[133]

Surprisingly, the 84th had only three men wounded in both the battles of Lookout Mountain and Missionary Ridge.[134] The North had driven back the Confederate forces, the supply lines had been opened, and the siege of Chattanooga was ended in dramatic fashion. Grant's daring plan had succeeded.

Lookout Mountain

Winter Quarters and a Gift from Home

During warmer months, troops typically slept in canvas tents or under the stars. But in the winter, "large camps were established with more substantial shelter."[135] Winter quarters were constructed of whatever was available, including trees, mud, leaves, and canvas. "These huts usually included a chimney, which kept the small space warm."[136] It was like building a temporary town.

Between the fall of 1863 and the winter of 1863-64, Joshua's Regiment had to construct winter quarters a total of four times.[137] Such was the life of a soldier in a war of shifting battle lines and changing strategy during a time of limited communication and ability to spot enemy troops. The hard, physical labor required to make even one winter quarters cannot be overstated. There were bright spots, though.

On December 7th and 8th, 1863, the boys from Mercer County received a welcome visitor from back home. "[T]he Rev. Mr. Chase, of Macomb, Illinois visited our camp and was cordially welcomed by many friends in

31

our Regiment. . . . On Sunday he consented to preach in our camp and delivered a very able and interesting address, which was listened to with profound attention by all."[138]

This visit was followed by receipt of an even greater morale booster—a shipment of food from home. "About Christmas quite a large number of barrels of onions, pickles and sour kraut, and boxes containing dried beef, butter, preserves, etc., etc., were received by members of our Regiment from home."[139] The shipment may have looked like onions, pickles and sauerkraut, but it was actually barrels and crates full of much needed home-grown encouragement and love. "[T]hey never will be able to realize how thankfully such favors as those above mentioned were received."[140]

CHAPTER SEVEN

Four Months in Hades—The Atlanta Campaign

THE WINTER OF 1863-64 HAD been devoted to preparing and strategizing for an assault on the Gate City of the South—the Confederate stronghold of Atlanta. The Union turned Nashville and Chattanooga into huge supply depots for the upcoming campaign. It is important to distinguish between the Battle of Atlanta (part of which is also referred to as the Siege of Atlanta) and the Atlanta Campaign which led up to it. The campaign lasted from May 6th to September 2nd, 1864. It was a long, grueling, and bloody endeavor. To say it was four months of hell is an understatement, because the fighting was nearly constant. The physical stamina and strength of heart Joshua and his Regiment must have had in order to endure four months of fighting and marching in the Southern heat are almost beyond comprehension.

The Atlanta Campaign was a prolonged chess match of military strategy and maneuvering by Commanding General Ulysses S. Grant and Major General Tecumseh Sherman, who was commanding the three armies of the campaign for the Union. One of Sherman's armies at this point was the Army of the Cumberland under General Thomas, which now included Joshua's 84th Illinois Infantry Regiment.

An initial objective of Sherman was to cut off Confederate General Joe Johnston's Army of Tennessee from his supply base in Atlanta. A similar tactic was used by Sherman throughout the campaign. He would use a portion of the Union forces to challenge Confederate defenses in order to hold them in place while the remainder of his troops maneuvered behind the ridges that characterized Northern Georgia in order to get around the

Confederate troops and cut them off. The Confederate Army would hold their lines until faced with being cut off and would then "quietly withdraw under cover of darkness to their next defensive line closer to Atlanta."[141]

Buzzard's Roost Gap and the Battle of Resaca

Joshua and his Regiment were involved from the beginning of the Atlanta campaign until the end. Their first target was the Confederates' strong defensive position in the steep ridges near Dalton, Georgia.[142] The crucial Western and Atlantic Railroad passed through the Rocky Face Ridge there via Buzzard's Roost Gap. The gap was protected by Confederate artillery positions along the ridge.[143] On May 8th and 9th, 1864, General Thomas attacked the gap with three divisions. Their efforts kept the main body of the Confederate troops occupied defending the ridges while other Union troops maneuvered to cut them off from their vital rail link at Resaca. Seeing this threat, the Rebels fell back to regroup at Resaca.[144]

Less than a week later, on May 14th and 15th, all the troops of both sides were jointly engaged for the first time in the Atlanta campaign at the Battle of Resaca. The two-day battle was largely a stalemate. However, during the battle Sherman sent a force across the Oostanaula River to threaten a Confederate supply line. The tactic worked, as the Confederates once again fell back to positions closer to Atlanta.[145]

On May 27th Joshua's Regiment fought in the Battle of Dallas.[146] However, it may have been difficult to tell when one battle ended and the next began. The fighting went on and on. As of early June, "The fight . . . still continued almost without cessation, and day after day, we were losing men, and apparently making very slow progress towards Atlanta."[147]

Kennesaw Mountain

The conflicts and maneuvers continued until the Southern forces pulled back to Kennesaw Mountain where they had strong defensive positions.[148] On June 27th Sherman boldly ordered a frontal assault on Kennesaw Mountain. The decision would prove costly. "Union troops fought their way up the hill but were repelled at the crest by artillery positions that had been hidden. . . . [T]he attack . . . cost 3000 casualties in less than an hour with no penetration of the defenses."[149] Although the direct attack on Kennesaw Mountain failed, Union troops succeeded in capturing a key road junction, once again forcing the Confederates to retreat.

Respite on the Chattahoochee

Sherman's forces followed the retreating Confederates, crossing the Chattahoochee River[150] north of Atlanta. After crossing, the Union army stopped there to regain strength for the assault on Atlanta that all knew was coming. This was a cherished time for Joshua and his Regiment. "On the tenth [of July], our Corps crossed the Chattahootchie River, and encamped upon a high bluff."[151] They would be joined by thousands more. "The whole army in the course of a week, encamped along the river to enjoy a slight respite from the severe labors of the campaign ere the assault was made upon a strongly fortified city of Atlanta."[152] This brief rest, which lasted until July 18th, was much needed and much appreciated by the men. "Never was a few days rest more imperiously required, or gratefully received by an army. . . . The men were very much wearied and worn down by the tremendous amount of labor, they had in so many successive weeks been required to perform."[153]

The energy expended in this protracted period of fighting, and the men's ability to keep going day after day is difficult to fathom. To make conditions even more unbearable, they were in the Deep South in July. The "heat during most of the day was insufferably intense."[154] The human spirit is indominable, however, and the young men took advantage of the opportunity the river presented. "Each morning and evening, hundreds flocked to banks of the river, and in swimming and fishing, were as gay and light hearted as any group of school boys could be enjoying a holiday or vacation."[155]

The Battle of Atlanta

As the Confederates retreated, the two armies continued moving closer and closer to Atlanta. A series of battles were fought around Atlanta as the

Union forces tried to sever the supply routes into the city. One of these was the Battle of Peachtree Creek on July 20th, 1864. When Sherman sent the Armies of the Ohio and the Tennessee east of Atlanta to attack the rail lines at Decatur, the Army of the Cumberland under Major General Thomas was left alone.[156] Confederate General John Bell Hood decided to take advantage of the opportunity to try to cut off and destroy Thomas's army as it crossed Peachtree Creek. Fortunately for Joshua and the 84th Illinois Infantry, Hood's attack was delayed and the Union army had already crossed the creek and was ready for the attack.[157] After two hours of fighting without a change in the lines, night was approaching. Hood then pulled off reserve troops to assist in defending against a Union advance further east and the battle ended.

At last, Atlanta was in the Union Army's sights. The warring that followed can only be described as hellacious. Known as the Siege of Atlanta, it lasted from July 22nd to August 25th. "From this time, for more than four weeks the bombardment of Atlanta was incessantly continued."[158] The noise alone was terrific. It was produced by "terribly shrieking elongated rifle shot, and our unceasing shower of terror-inspiring shells and shrapnel."[159] The onslaught was unremitting. "Generally, from sunset until far into the night, there was a deep and at times almost deafening thunder of artillery, playing upon the doomed city."[160] In the end, Atlanta, the "Gate City of the South," fell to the Union forces. But the fighting was not yet over.

Joshua's Regiment made a flank movement on Jonesboro until August 30th, followed by the Battle of Jonesboro from August 31st to September 1st. They were next engaged at Lovejoy Station from September 2nd to 6th. Finally, the fighting ended. "The great campaign was now completed. For four months the crack and rattle of musketry, and the fearful thunder of heavy artillery had scarcely ceased. For four months our men had been engaged in building line after line of breastworks and slowly, yet surely forcing the enemy back."[161] Atlanta was finally in their possession, but not without great cost. Joshua's Regiment lost 12 men killed and 77 wounded, of whom six more died.[162]

Battle flag of the 84th Illinois Infantry Regiment

CHAPTER EIGHT

From the Brink of Surrender to Victory:
The Battles of Franklin and Nashville

THE MONTHS FOLLOWING THE ATLANTA campaign were initially free of the intense fighting that Joshua and his comrades had just endured. The Regiment did, however, conduct operations against Confederate General John Bell Hood in North Georgia and North Alabama from September 29th to November 3rd. These months may have been free of major battles, but unfortunately, they were also free of pay for Joshua and his Regiment. This was a great hardship on the families back home. Finally, on November 16th the Paymaster arrived at camp.[163]

The enemy had by no means surrendered, though. And life was still hard for the troops. Joshua and his Regiment were now headed back to Tennessee. The number of miles they marched across the South is truly amazing. "[O]n the evening of the 24th [of November], our Brigade marched thirty-three miles within thirteen hours, without halting for rest or refreshment, and more than half the distance carrying on a skirmish with the enemy's cavalry."[164]

No state more so than Tennessee witnessed shifting lines of control by the two opposing armies. In late November 1863, Joshua would bear witness to this and also to a particularly moving sight. When his Regiment reached the Duck River in the central part of the state, "The wagon trains were immediately sent across . . . where there were thousands of negroes already assembled . . . who were making their exodus from the fluctuating borders of the Southern Confederacy."[165] The sight of thousands of fleeing slaves must have been both shocking and inspiring to the Union troops. Although Confederate General Hood's forces were now advancing into Tennessee, Joshua and his Regiment would continue fighting to make sure the fleeing refugees did not fall back into slavery.

The Battle of Franklin

One of the more harrowing experiences during Joshua's many battles occurred during the Battle of Franklin. Hood's goal was to cut off and destroy the Army of the Cumberland before it could reach the rest of the Union Army in Nashville.[166] He nearly succeeded, as Joshua's Regiment was in fact cut off. And in this precarious position, the Regiment was only hours from imminent slaughter or surrender. After the glory of Stones River, Lookout Mountain, and Missionary Ridge, and after the hard-fought triumph at Atlanta, an ignominious end nearly came to the Illinois 84th one night at Franklin. The anguish of Joshua and the other men during that fateful night can only be partially understood. All they had suffered and endured would have been for naught if some miracle did not save them from their predicament. "Our position was now one of terrible suspense. . . . [A]n immensely superior force was only waiting till dawn of day to renew the attack, having already cut us off from the other Divisions of the Corps. . . . Every man now realized that unless succor came within a few hours, a surrender was inevitable."[167] But the Union was not to lose the 84th after all. "About one o'clock, sharp skirmish firing commenced on the road toward Columbia, and a joyful yet suppressed cheer instantly ran through the town. We knew that a force was coming—could it possibly reach us! Soon the firing ceased, and General Ruger's Division . . . began to pass by."[168] Joshua's Regiment had been saved.

Overall, the battle of Franklin was a disaster for the Confederates. General Hood's decision to order a full-frontal assault on strong Union positions resulted in catastrophic losses—six of his generals and nearly a third of his men. Still not deterred, Hood pushed on towards Nashville for a final showdown.

The Battle of Nashville

Having endured the heat of Georgia the previous summer, the 84th was now about to experience the dread chill of winter out-of-doors. It was December, but this year they would not be in winter quarters. The battle for Nashville was about to begin. "The prelude to the Battle of Nashville was the drive into central Tennessee by Hood's Army of Tennessee in late November 1864."[169] Even though he had experienced heavy casualties at Franklin, Hood proceeded to the outskirts of Nashville, inviting confrontation in the dead of winter. After the Battle of Franklin, "the weather set in very cold, a slight snow fell, and then rain and sleet in succession, and the entire surface of the ground was covered in ice."[170] These were horrendous conditions for war. But war came, nonetheless.

On the morning of December 15th, the supply wagons of Joshua's Regiment were loaded and sent to the rear.[171] "[T]he men had all their accoutrements on or ready to be put on at a moment's notice, and thus in readiness, waited until about daylight, before the final orders came to move."[172] The scene was reminiscent of the Continental Army crossing the Delaware on another December morning 88 years prior. "The morning was so dark and foggy, that the movements of our forces were completely concealed from the enemy."[173] Still, what lay ahead was daunting. The Confederates held fortified positions between the Union forces and Nashville and overtaking these positions would be anything but certain. Yet, the North would prevail. And it did so in dramatic fashion. In the decisive hours of the battle, "The Army of the Cumberland surged out of its trenches and overwhelmed the Confederate Army."[174] Even the Union soldiers were amazed at the success. "Forcing the enemy back from their fortified position in front of Nashville was certainly one of the most scientific and brilliant achievements of the war."[175]

Unlike some of the previous battles, this time the 84th did not suffer serious casualties in the two-day battle—quite the opposite. "Our Regiment though closely engaged on both days, did not have a man killed, and had only five or six seriously wounded."[176] The Battle of Nashville had been won for the Union and, once again, Joshua survived. For his family back in Illinois, the news of the victories at Franklin and Nashville had to have been encouraging. Still, they had no way of knowing when or if Joshua would make it back home. Christmas would once again be spent apart. From December 20th to the 28th, Joshua and the Union troops pursued the retreating Confederates south to the Tennessee River in Alabama.[177]

Battle of Nashville Monument.
Photo by Steve Grasz

CHAPTER NINE

Winter in Alabama

JOSHUA AND THE 84TH ILLINOIS were next ordered to proceed to Huntsville, Alabama to build winter quarters in that once prosperous, but now occupied, Appalachian city. Since the autumn of 1863, Huntsville had served as a base for Union operations. It was a strategic location as it controlled access to the Memphis and Charleston Railroad. By January 6th, 1865, Joshua and the 84th Illinois had encamped near Huntsville and were constructing quarters for the winter. However, a big surprise was in store.

Guarding the Occupied City

"Our Regiment had made considered progress in building log huts and shanties, when the astonishing news came, that the 84th Regiment, Illinois Volunteers, had been selected as Provost Guard of the city."[178] Joshua and his Company H got the news on the morning of January 9th and that same day he moved into Huntsville and encamped with his Regiment in the courthouse square.[179] That was the good news. The bad news was this meant construction would start again on their winter quarters.

In a letter sent home from Huntsville just after their arrival on January 9th, 1865, Joshua's fellow Company H member John Webster Dilley wrote to his sister, Mary (who would later become Joshua's wife):

> I am in hopes we will get to remain here for a few weeks till
> we get some rest for we are all very much fatigued from the
> marching and fighting we have done. Since . . . the 2nd of

August we have marched 800 miles and have been in three
hard battles and were in the siege of Atlanta besides which
was a fight nearly all the time it lasted.[180]

A surprising aspect of the letter is that it indicates correspondence
must have been limited, given that the Atlanta Campaign had ended
several months prior. Dilley wrote that the regiment was quartered in the
courthouse until their barracks could be built.[181] A historic photograph
of Huntsville's courthouse square occupied by the 84th Illinois Infantry
Regiment documents this.

Dilley's letter also described Huntsville in flattering terms. "Huntsville
is a nice town the finest I think I have seen in the south. It is finely situated.
The buildings are well constructed and the inhabitants many of them have
been wealthy previous to the war."[182] John Webster Dilley's letter to his sister
survived and was passed on in Mary and Joshua's family for generations.[183]

John Webster Dilley

Once settled, the 84th Illinois Regiment proceeded to construct shanties
on the south half of the courthouse square, using lumber taken from barns
and unoccupied homes in and near the city.[184] The shelters were modest,

but all had fireplaces and chimneys. The officers of the Regiment, however, found rooms in the courthouse which they fitted up for their quarters.[185]

On January 10th, 1865, one of the most valiant and battle-tested regiments in the Union Army began their new and unfamiliar assignment keeping order as Provost Guard of the occupied city of Huntsville. Anyone who saw them in those first few days, however, would have seen a raggedy crew in battle-scarred uniforms rather than anything resembling a polished provost guard. Joshua and his Regiment had not been supplied with clothes since December 4th—long before the Battle of Nashville.[186] "During the battle [of Nashville] as well as while in pursuit of General Hood, and on the subsequent march, the men had torn and worn out their clothing so badly, that in our Regiment, when detailed for provost duty, there were scarcely enough of whole clothes to be found, to supply the detail who daily patrolled the streets."[187] This would soon be remedied. On January 15th the Regiment received new uniforms.[188]

84th Illinois Infantry Regiment at the Madison County
Alabama Courthouse, January 1865.
Huntsville-Madison County Public Library Special
Collections. Used by permission.

A somewhat amusing, but perhaps predictable, result of turning a battle-hardened regiment into a military police force is that they tolerated no breach of decorum in the city—even by much surprised Union officers on leave.[189]

Joshua, who had now risen to the rank of Sergeant, and his Company H would continue their stint as military police in Huntsville until March. On the 12th of that month, they received orders to move by rail to Knoxville, Tennessee. They arrived on March 14th, and from there the Regiment went on an expedition to Bull's Gap and conducted operations in East Tennessee for over a month.

CHAPTER TEN

A Time to Dance and a Time to Mourn

For everything there is a season, and a time for every purpose under heaven: a time to be born, and a time to die; a time to plant, and a time to pluck up what is planted; a time to kill, and a time to heal; a time to break down, and a time to build up; a time to weep and a time to laugh; a time to mourn and a time to dance.[190]

ONE CAN ONLY SUPPOSE THESE well-known lines of scripture came to the mind of Joshua during the tumultuous events of April 1865.

Just a month earlier, on March 4th, President Lincoln had delivered his second inaugural address. The country was both processing the devastation of the war and praying for its end. Newspapers of the day communicated Lincoln's soul-piercing words to the troops, including his final paragraphs:

Fondly do we hope—fervently do we pray—that this mighty scourge of war may speedily pass away. . . .

With malice toward none with charity for all with firmness in the right as God gives us to see the right let us strive on to finish the work we are in to bind up the nation's wounds, to care for him who shall have borne the battle and for his widow and his orphan—to do all which may achieve and cherish a just and lasting peace among ourselves and with all nations.[191]

Lincoln's prayer for a speedy end to the war was soon answered. On April 10th, the news of Confederate General Robert E. Lee's surrender to Union General Grant the previous day at Appomattox Court House in Virginia reached Joshua and the 84th Regiment. The celebration was immediate and ecstatic. "[T]he loud shouts, and cheers of joy and triumph, rung and reverberated from camp to camp."[192] The jubilation was soon followed by dreams of a quick return home. "Bright visions of a speedy, and joyful return to the homes of our childhood, to the embrace of our beloved kindred, arose before the minds of thousands of war-worn soldiers."[193] There was also a deep sense of relief from a painful national reckoning. Lincoln had just delivered the sobering and convicting prophesy to the nation that God may intend for the offense of slavery to be removed by the mighty scourge of war "until every drop of blood drawn with the lash shall be paid by another drawn with the sword." At last, it was finished.

Now, it was time to give thanks to God for the war's end and the victory won. April 14th was set aside as a day of thanksgiving throughout the Union Army and the whole country.[194] "[T]he day, if not devoted to prayer and praise with the lips, was consecrated in the hearts of those who had borne the brunt and shock of battle, in defense of their beloved country."[195]

The praise and thanksgiving, however, as well as the jubilation, would soon turn to mourning—very soon. The next day, April 15th, 1865, just 41 days after the president's second inauguration, Joshua and his Regiment learned of the assassination of President Abraham Lincoln. It was a gut punch as painful to the men as the rout at Chickamauga. The news "sent a chill of dread through the stalwart frames of thousands who had faced the cannons mouth undaunted, producing an almost benumbed sensation of horror and dismay."[196] Joshua and his fellow 84th Illinois Volunteers had marched many hundreds of miles and fought battle after bloody battle across the South to preserve the Union under the leadership of their home state President only to have a Confederate assassin steal the joy of their hard-won victory. Though Lincoln was gone, they knew in their hearts that, as sung in the Battle Hymn of the Republic, "his truth is marching on." The Union had been saved and millions of enslaved human beings had been set free.

CHAPTER ELEVEN

Mustered Out of Service

On April 21st, 1865, Joshua boarded a train bound for Nashville via Knoxville and Chattanooga.[197] He arrived in Nashville on the 23rd. Like many things in the army, perhaps, the end of his service came with deliberate speed—that is with much waiting. Finally, on the 8th of June 1865, Joshua was mustered out of service to the United States.[198] Before departing for their homes, the men of the 84th Regiment were given a hero's farewell address by General Nathan Kimball who had served as a division commander during the Battles of Franklin and Nashville. Kimball's words echo through the ages:

> [A]fter three years of gallant devotion to the cause of our common country, in this war against rebellion, you are now about to return to your homes with honor unsullied, and with reputations bright with glory. Your deeds will live on forever. In nearly every battle of the Southwest, you have been engaged: at Perryville, Stones River, Chickamauga, Lookout Mountain, Missionary Ridge, Resaca, Rocky Face, Dallas, New Hope Church, Kenesaw, Jonesboro, Lovejoy, Atlanta, Franklin and Nashville you have borne the flag of the Union and the banner of your noble State, to victory over the foe who would have destroyed the Government made by our fathers.[199]

Joshua was about to depart uniformed service to his country, but he would continue to cherish and honor the flag of the Union throughout his life.

Home Sweet Home—Return to the Prairie State and Land of Lincoln

On June 9th, Joshua boarded a train in Nashville bound for Louisville, arriving there late that night.[200] The next day, Joshua and his Regiment marched down to Portland, Kentucky (today a neighborhood of Louisville), where they boarded another train and crossed the Ohio River into Indiana.[201] The men could not help but be saddened by the realization that only 346 of them would cross back out of the 932 "who were our comrades in crossing some thirty-two months before."[202] According to the Illinois Adjutant General's Report, the 84th Illinois Infantry had a total of 689 casualties from battle, disease, and accident.[203]

A Hero's Welcome

Joshua had marched many hundreds of miles through Kentucky, Tennessee, Georgia, and Alabama—most of these states more than once. For three years he had fought and lived in the forested valleys and mountains of Dixie, never seeing his beloved prairie. Nor were he and his comrades close enough to feel the admiration and support of the folks back home. Those things were about to change.

The train was now heading north in the general direction of Illinois by way of Lafayette, Indiana. The men were already in great spirits at the prospect of going home. But what happened next must have seemed like a dream to Joshua and his companions. The scene was one of great emotion, patriotism, and pride. "Soon after sunrise . . . we began to realize we were again in 'God's country.' Hundreds flocked to the depots at every station we passed, and scarfs and handkerchiefs were waved at every house near the Railroad."[204] It was a triumphant return from a hard-fought victory. "They waived us a 'welcome home' and the boys reported by a rousing cheer, as at each house and station, the loyal inhabitants rushed forth to salute 'the loyal, true and brave.'"[205]

Joshua and his comrades were soon to see another welcome sight. "About fifty miles south of Lafayette, we came out of the rough timbered country, upon a broad prairie, and in a moment a long ringing cheer arose from the whole Regiment. It was the first true PRAIRIE we had seen for many months, and strongly reminded all, that we were approaching our beloved and beautiful Prairie State."[206]

On June 12th, the Regiment's train crossed into Illinois. It continued to Camp Butler near Springfield where they encamped. It was a joyful time, yet the next day brought a dose of disappointment. The Regiment had planned to march through Springfield, to Oak Ridge Cemetery, "to visit the grave of the beloved and lamented President Lincoln. . . . [B]ut a storm came on in the morning, and continued most of the day, so we were deprived of the opportunity of paying a deserved tribute to the Soldier's Friend and Nation's Preserver."[207]

On the 16th Joshua and his fellow volunteers returned all their military property, got their final pay, and were discharged.[208] They had lived, marched, and fought together for three years and through some of the bloodiest and most historic battles and campaigns of the Civil War.

The 84th Illinois Infantry Regiment had earned its considerable acclaim. "Its hard-earned fame will be handed down to future generations untarnished, unobscured; and in the minds and hearts of the true patriots of the State of Illinois, it will ever be known as one of the best, most intrepid and unflinching, of the many noble regiments who went forth to succor and save the best Government, that mortal wisdom and patriotism has ever established."[209]

The source of the 84th Illinois Infantry Regiment's valor and prominence on the battlefield can be attributed to several things. The Regiment's own soldier-historian noted the superior discipline learned in early drilling and training. One can also point to the fact the men of the Regiment were already steeled and strong from life on the Illinois prairie. Hard physical work was nothing new. Neither were building living quarters from limited resources or relying on firearms for food and security. The Regiment's early experience with brutal conditions in the Kentucky snow may also have given the Regiment an especially intense loyalty and determination not to let the suffering of their fallen comrades be in vain. And, consistent with the remarks of President Lincoln just weeks before his death during his Second Inaugural Address, the bravery, endurance, and ultimate success of the 84th may be seen as part of their mortal but providential role in the righteous judgment of God on the evil of slavery.

Joshua Brown's G.A.R. medal in recognition of service in the Civil War.
Photo by Steve Grasz

CHAPTER TWELVE

Love of a Lady, the Land, and the Law

Joshua returned to Mercer County, Illinois, as a war hero, but with the war's end it was time to return to the family farm and start thinking about a family of his own. Joshua left home a twenty-one-year-old farm boy and returned a war-hardened veteran. Yet, he was still just 24, and the resiliency of youth is perhaps stronger even than war. There was so much to be done. Joshua had been gone from the farm for years and his father, Benjamin, had not been able to keep up with all the work without his help.

For the nation, there were much bigger challenges than deferred farm work. Well over 600,000 men had died in the war.[210] Thousands more were wounded or disabled. This meant there were literally millions of widows, orphans, and heart-broken parents, siblings, and grandparents. The nation needed healing physically, emotionally, and spiritually. As Lincoln had exhorted near the end of the war, "let us strive to finish the work we are in; to bind up the nation's wounds; to care for him who shall have borne the battle, and his widow, and his orphan."[211]

Time does heal, and before long a young lady named Mary, the sister of his Company H comrade, John Webster Dilley, caught Joshua's eye. Less than 18 months after his return from the war Joshua and Mary were united in marriage on January 1st, 1867. Mary was 22 years old at the time of their wedding.[212] The New Year's Day ceremony was conducted "at the residence of the officiating clergyman."[213]

To put the historical setting of their wedding into context, it is interesting to note that the week before Joshua and Mary's wedding announcement appeared in print, the same local newspaper carried the headline "Horrible

Indian Massacre." With a dateline of Omaha, the story related the killing of all 80-plus soldiers from the 18ᵗʰ U.S. Infantry by 3,000 Sioux, Cheyenne, and Arapaho warriors, led by legendary Lakota Chief Red Cloud, near Fort Phil Kearny in Wyoming on December 21ˢᵗ.[214] For the time being, Illinois was a much safer place for a family than the western frontier.

Now married, Joshua and Mary started a home and began farming there in Mercer County. Their home was in the southeast quarter of section 10 in Suez Township.[215] The farm was about seven miles south of Viola, Illinois, but the address would become North Henderson, which would be laid out as a town in 1871. Joshua's land was gently sloping, and the soil was dark and rich. Still, the early years would not be easy. In May of 1867, their first corn crop was threatened by continued heavy rains at planting time.[216] The work was hard, but there was occasionally time for fun. After some prompting from the local paper,[217] county residents planned a patriotic celebration for the Fourth of July.

In "Dickens's" terms, 1870 would prove to be the best of times and the worst of times for the young couple. "From early April to the first of July, there was not, in Aledo and its vicinity, sufficient rain, at any one time, to moisten the earth an inch in depth."[218] "The heat was intense, the mercury, for over a week, ranging from 98 degrees to 104 degrees, in the shade, during the heat of the day."[219] The prairie grass was "as brown as in mid winter."[220] The prospects for corn and other crops was bleak and a late freeze had already doomed the bounty of most fruit trees. Still, being the patriotic people they were, the Fourth of July was again celebrated with gusto. "Early in the morning the people from the country came pouring into [Aledo], in large numbers, which continued throughout the forenoon."[221]

What Joshua and Mary would remember about 1870, though, was not the hardships caused by the severe drought. Nearly three years had passed since their marriage without starting a family. That would now change. Following completion of the meager corn harvest and just before Christmas, a daughter came into the world on December 19ᵗʰ, 1870. She was named Vinnie Ream. Their farmstead was filled with joy and the cries of a newborn. Of course, the family now had a child to support and the corn crop (what little there was of it that year) was worth only 25 cents a bushel.[222] By spring, though, it would be worth a more respectable 40 cents.[223] In addition to improved crop prices, 1871 would also bring plentiful spring rains and the Brown family's prospects improved. By the end of May, the "stand of Corn was never better than at present."[224]

Planting, cultivating, and harvesting continued their annual cycles. More than seven years would pass with no other child being born. Mary and Joshua must have wondered whether their first child would be their last. However, the couple would eventually be blessed with a total of seven children! Their second child, this time a son, Cyrus Dilley (Cy), was born on April 11th, 1878. Another son, Gus Bruington, would follow more quickly on July 29th, 1879. These two were born during a unique time in the lives of Joshua and Mary. Joshua was entering another period of public service. Although Joshua had always been a farmer, he decided to put his Provost Guard experience from the war to use in public office. In August of 1878, he was nominated by the Mercer County Republican Party at their convention in Aledo to run as their candidate for County Sherriff. He then campaigned for the office that fall.[225]

On November 5th, 1878, Joshua was elected as the Sheriff of Mercer County. It was a three-way partisan race (the Republican, Democrat, and Greenback parties each fielded a nominee) and Joshua captured 50% of the vote. He received 1772 votes, a margin of 845 over the second-place candidate.[226]

Joshua and his family moved from their farm at the southeast corner of the county to the county seat of Aledo during this time. Joshua's salary was $1,320 a year. Sheriffs also received additional fees for performing certain services.[227] Joshua named his old Company H war buddy and now brother-in-law, John Webster Dilley, as Deputy Sheriff.

Joshua served a single two-year term in 1879 and 1880. Perhaps Mercer County was not quite the wild west by this time, but in many ways it remained so. The *Aledo Times Record* later described Joshua as a "pioneer sheriff."[228] Some of the challenges he faced are familiar even to county sheriffs today. At the 1879 Mercer County Fair, there were so many "penny swindlers" doing business on the fairgrounds that the editor of the local paper denounced the lot as "one grand gambling den."[229] Other duties were more mundane. These included conducting sheriff's sales of tax delinquent land,[230] and transporting prisoners. In February of 1880, "Sheriff Brown took the three prisoners confined in jail for violation of [a] Village Ordinance . . . to Cambridge, Henry County to appear before Judge Glenn in an attempt to secure their release through the medium of a writ of habeas corpus."[231] The judge denied their request and "the trio were remanded to jail . . . poorer, sadder, and no doubt wiser than when they started away."[232]

Another incident that seems quite humorous now, but which was decidedly not funny to Joshua, occurred in late September of 1879. "Sheriff Brown was made the victim of misplaced confidence on Saturday evening last. He gave Tom McFarland permission to go to the cistern after a bucket of water, and as he has not yet returned, it is supposed that he couldn't find the cistern. The Sheriff will pay $50 for his re-arrest and return."[233] It is not known whether the prisoner was ever re-captured.

A plaque listing Joshua's name as Sheriff of Mercer County hangs in the Sheriff's office in Aledo, Illinois today.

After his term was completed, Joshua returned to farming and he was not on the ballot in 1880. Life returned to the familiar rhythm of the seasons on the farm. Their fourth child, a son named Joshua Logan, was born on August 9th, 1883. A second daughter, Vernice Claire, was born there in Mercer County on August 2nd, 1887. Upon Vernice's birth, the local paper reported that "Ex-Sheriff J.H. Brown is supremely happy and a broad smile overspreads his countenance. It is a girl. Father and mother are doing as well as can be expected."[234] Another daughter, Lucinda Mabel, was born in 1888, but like so many children during that era, did not survive.

Mercer County Court House, Aledo, Illinois.
Photo by Steve Grasz

CHAPTER THIRTEEN

Home on the Range

Joshua and Mary Settle the Nebraska Frontier

PART OF WHAT MAKES JOSHUA Hobbs Brown an especially notable American figure is that after more than four decades of pioneering on the Illinois prairie and after his heroic service in the Civil War he set out on yet another adventure that also changed the course of history.

Joshua was well situated after the war. He was married with several young children and had been engaged in farming on his own land in Mercer County for nearly 20 years. He was a respected member of the community and had even served a stint in elected office. In 1884, however, Joshua suffered the loss of his father, Benjamin Franklin Brown, who died suddenly of heart failure on August 24.[235]

Grave of Benjamin Franklin Brown and Lucinda Mann
Brown, Mann Cemetery in Mercer County, Illinois.
Photo by Steve Grasz

In addition to losing his father, a new threat soon faced Joshua and his family—the "white plague," better known as tuberculosis or "consumption." During the 19th century, tuberculosis was the leading cause of death in the United States and "one of the most dreaded diseases known to mankind."[236] It is not likely Joshua actually contracted the disease, as it was often fatal within a few years. However, records from a census taken of Civil War veterans reveals that Joshua suffered lung damage during the war (perhaps from breathing gun powder smoke almost continuously for months during the Atlanta campaign). He apparently either had symptoms that caused a health scare or was concerned he would contract the disease due to his weakened lungs.[237] In any event, having seen the devastation of disease among his comrades during the Kentucky campaign and throughout the war, Joshua was not about to take the matter lightly. Joshua, like others at that time, decided to move to the drier climate of Nebraska for his health. In the fall of 1885, Joshua and Mary began selling their Illinois land. One sixteen-acre parcel (perhaps a timber lot) was sold to his younger brother, Samuel M. Brown, for $400.[238] That November, Joshua journeyed west and filed a homestead claim in the Nebraska panhandle.[239] The claim was located at Section 18, Township 13, Range 44 in what was then Cheyenne County.[240]

Three years later, at age 47 (somewhat "over the hill" in those days since the average life expectancy was less than 44 years) Joshua started out on a new and historic adventure. He took his growing family and headed west, joining many other Civil War veterans in the great westward expansion. But Joshua and Mary and their family did not just move to Nebraska; they moved to the Nebraska panhandle in the far west. The difference between Eastern and Western Nebraska at this time in history was the difference between civilization and the wild west. Western movie buffs may recall a scene from *The Cowboys*, starring John Wayne. When a young cowboy asked if the upcoming cattle drive would require long hard days— even on Sundays—he was famously told, "There ain't no Sundays west of Omaha!"[241]

In 1860, only 28,841 people lived in the entire Nebraska Territory. The western areas were still controlled and occupied by fierce nomadic tribes including the Sioux, Cheyenne, and Arapaho. After president Lincoln signed the Homestead Act on May 20th, 1862, granting 160 acres of land to brave souls willing to homestead on the frontier, settlers began moving to the eastern part of Nebraska. However, Western Nebraska was a different story.

In 1865, while Joshua was completing his military service in Alabama and Tennessee, Western Nebraska Territory and Northeastern Colorado

Territory were also at war. Just miles south of the site of Joshua's future Nebraska homestead, the Battle of Julesburg took place on January 7th, 1865. One thousand Cheyenne, Arapaho and Lakota Sioux warriors attacked 60 soldiers and 40-50 civilians at Julesburg and nearby Fort Sedgwick, killing 14 soldiers and four civilians. Fort Sedgwick, at the confluence of the South Platte River and Lodgepole Creek, had been established in 1864 to protect against Indian attacks on overland trail pioneers heading west by wagon train to Oregon and California. The fort was abandoned in 1871 and the military presence in the area shifted to Fort Sidney, about 30 miles west, also along the Lodgepole Creek. Fort Sidney (originally called Sidney Barracks) had its beginning in 1867. By 1875 it had quarters for three companies, plus five officers' quarters and a hospital. The last "Indian alarm" at the fort came in 1878.

In addition to the Homestead Act, Congress had passed the Timber Culture Act in 1873, offering additional land grants to settlers who agreed to plant trees on part of their land. However, the Pawnee and Ponca tribes still lived in Nebraska until 1875 and 1878, respectively, and in 1876, war with the Sioux still raged on Nebraska's northern border due to encroachment of gold seekers into the Black Hills. So, settlement in the far west was virtually non-existent. Several developments, however, rapidly changed the situation. For one thing, hostilities with the Native American tribes largely ceased after the late 1870s. Technology also played a role. A simple but transformational invention, barbed wire, came on the scene in 1874. This product allowed settlers to fence in the open range and separate livestock from crops. Finally, the completion of the Public Land Survey of the area was accomplished by 1880. Western Nebraska was now open to settlement. The transcontinental railroad had been completed through Nebraska in 1867, but now it was relatively safe to travel by rail even in the far west.

Settlers who came to central and eastern parts of Nebraska in the 1870s faced swarms of grasshoppers from 1874 to 1877. These voracious insects ruined crops and sent many homesteaders back east in defeat. However, since half of the total labor force in the U.S. was comprised of farmers, the demand for farmland was still high and another wave of settlers took their place in the early 1880s. "By the year 1880 the people . . . started to settle the western half of the state which was at that time nearly all wild land."[242] The area was in rapid transition. Cheyenne County had been formed, consisting of the entire southern Nebraska panhandle—an area 50 miles wide and 102 miles in length, encompassing 5,100 square miles.[243] This state-sized wild west county (larger than Connecticut) was where the Browns were headed. The entire county, from the Wyoming border east, had but 190 residents in 1870 and only 1,558 by 1880.[244]

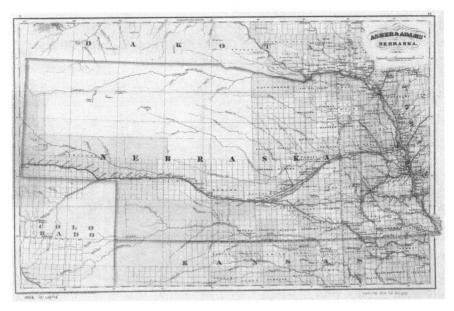

Map of Nebraska showing unsettled areas.
Library of Congress, Geography and Map Division.

A New Life in a New State, a Newly Formed County, and a New Town

It was the spring of 1888 when Joshua and the Brown family left the green fields of Illinois for good and moved to the treeless plains of Nebraska to homestead near the nascent town of Chappell.[245] The main line of the Union Pacific Railroad ran right through Chappell (and had brought the town into existence). So, Joshua and his family planned to head west by rail. Little did they know, the moving process would take months. In late February of 1888, Joshua chartered a rail car and proceeded to load up what the family needed to homestead in Nebraska.[246] Unfortunately, his plans were about to be thrown into chaos. The engineers and firemen of the Chicago, Burlington, and Quincy Railroad were in a labor dispute and decided to go on strike. The "Burlington Railroad Strike of 1888" is regarded as "one of the most significant labor conflicts of the 19th century."[247] The strike drug on, seriously delaying the Brown's ability to establish their home and plant life-sustaining crops before it was too late in the season. On March 9th, 1888, the local paper there in Mercer County reported, "The effect of the strike of engineers and fireman is quite noticeable right here in Viola. Our merchants are almost out of sugar, flour, and oil. Mr. J.H. Brown has his household goods and farm implements loaded ready for shipment to Neb[raska]."[248] The same paper reported "both sides" of the labor dispute remained "resolute."[249] The situation was tense, and violence flared. "Few trains [were] running on the Q. road in Nebraska." And for good reason. Trains in Nebraska had been sabotaged, and explosives were discovered under tracks. "A non-union engineer was roughly handled by a mob at McCook, Neb[raska]." In fact, he was "beaten almost to death."[250] Weeks more passed. The family remained in Mercer County through the end of the month and finally headed west in April.[251]

Traveling by train may sound cushy for pioneers, and it certainly beat travelling cross country by covered wagon. However, it was not what it may seem. First of all, the trip was 700 long miles. And steam engines were loud and rough. They spewed thick clouds of black smoke from their coal fireboxes. Then there was the challenge of switching from the Chicago, Burlington, and Quincy Railroad to the Union Pacific for the last leg of the journey. There were no roads in the new land and no automobiles. The rail line was simply a conveyor belt to the edge of civilization.

It must have looked like Joshua had quite an entourage on the train behind that huge steam engine. The Browns were a family of seven, and in addition to some basic personal belongings they brought everything from horses and farm implements to tools and supplies needed to start homesteading in Nebraska. It was a long journey, but the family's anticipation grew as the train entered the great Platte River Valley for the last major segment of the journey. When the train chugged through Julesburg (just inside the not-yet-teenaged state of Colorado and only 16 miles from their stop at Chappell) Joshua and the family knew they had almost arrived. Within a few miles the tracks veered away from the South

Platte Valley and angled west-northwest up the Lodgepole Valley just to the north of the mouth of the Lodgepole Creek. This small and unassuming little stream would play a big role in their new lives on the prairie. It would be an initial source of water and later a favorite hunting spot and a place for the children to play and explore. Lodgepole Creek, so named because plains tribes followed it to its headwaters to secure teepee poles, is the longest creek in the United States, rising on the eastern slopes of the Laramie Mountains in Wyoming and running across the Nebraska Panhandle to merge with the South Platte River in Colorado.[252]

Mixed feelings of excitement, adventure, trepidation, and loss raced through the family members' minds as they neared their destination. It had to have been difficult for daughter Vinnie, then seventeen, to leave her friends in Illinois. All of the Browns had left loved ones behind. One member of the family, though, had no such cares. Joshua and Mary's youngest child, daughter Vernice, was less than a year old when she arrived in Nebraska.

When they finally set eyes on Chappell, one wonders if Mary could hide the apprehension in her heart from her countenance. A photograph of the town around that time shows the new settlement consisted of only a handful of wood frame buildings—and not a single tree in sight.[253] There was, however, at least one significant new building. A news article in 1886 had noted, "There are no vacant buildings in Chappell, and when settlers arrive, they find almost no place for storage of goods because we have such a small depot building. However, we have word that the U.P. Ry Co. intends to erect a commodious structure during the coming summer."[254] And so they did. The recently completed Union Pacific depot greeted Joshua as he and his family arrived.[255]

After deboarding the train, and perhaps decoupling the rail car, the family tended to their tired and bewildered horses and then off-loaded all their possessions. Next, they would have filled water barrels from a windmill at the train depot or perhaps from the Lodgepole Creek. They then gathered their children and left for their homestead by horse-drawn wagon, heading overland through native prairie. Their hearts were racing with anticipation and, for some, maybe even a little fear. There was no law enforcement other than Joshua's gun. The first county sheriff did not take office until the following January, and the nearest military outpost, Fort Sidney, was nearly 30 miles to the west—a day's journey by horse. Once they got to the homestead, there was no running water and, unless Joshua had performed advance work, no shelter. Everything from a water well to a home and a barn had to be constructed by hard, tedious labor with no electricity and no power tools. Even simple necessities were a challenge. With trees a precious and rare commodity, it is likely the Brown children gathered bundles of prairie grass and any available "cow chips" to help warm the family on cold nights and to save buying coal that had to be hauled by wagon from Chappell.

The herds of bison, once numbering in the millions, were gone, but not by long. Their bones could still be found and sold or used for fertilizer. Pronghorn antelope, however, still abounded on the Nebraska plains. These icons of the grasslands are the fastest mammals in the world over long distances. Even at short distances they are second only to the cheetah and can run at speeds of 55 or more miles per hour. Joshua and his family would also have encountered prairie chickens, black-tailed prairie dogs, jackrabbits, mule deer, burrowing owls, swift foxes, coyotes, and perhaps even an occasional prairie wolf. These wolves once roamed the plains in great numbers following the bison herds. The last siting of one of these wolves in Nebraska was in 1913. Rattlesnakes, capable of killing a child or an adult with its poisonous venom, were commonplace.

Despite the hardships, the area was exploding with new settlers, and it had to be an exciting time filled with hope, anticipation, and new friendships. In 1880, the population of the Big Springs Precinct of Cheyenne County, which included what would become the county encompassing the towns of Big Springs and Chappell, was just 99.[256] In 1884, Chappell "was only a railroad siding with a station house and one small shack."[257] This station house was "part dug out, railroad ties, and the wreck of an old freight car."[258] Things changed quickly. Between 1880 and 1890, the population of Nebraska soared from 452,402 to 1,062,656. Land was still being claimed under the Homestead and Timber Culture Acts. In addition, the Union Pacific Railroad had been granted large tracts of land across Nebraska to finance completion of the transcontinental railroad. The company owned every other section of land for twenty miles on both sides of the track.[259] The Union Pacific began selling this land in the Chappell area in 1884 and the town of Chappell was platted in August of that same year. By June of 1887, Chappell had a population of about 200, although no schoolhouse yet existed.[260] So, the Browns arrival in April of 1888 was amid rapid and historic change on the high plains.

In addition to an influx of Civil War veterans and their families from states such as Illinois, the settlement of Western Nebraska was being fueled by a westward migration of first-and second-generation European immigrants. Among the earliest settlers in the Chappell area were a number of Swedish families. Other early settlers included Germans and Mennonites[261] In the early years on their homestead, Joshua and Mary were part of a wider community of pioneers that included names such as Carlson, Wolf, Moline, McAuliffe, Babcock, Stutzman, Guenin, Grasz, Wertz, Sudman, Zehr, Soderquist, Cooper, and Paulsen. They were soon joined by such family names as LaSelle,[262] Johnson, Kalb, Shunk, Yoder, Bower, Freeman, Cave, Cheleen, Smith, Akeson, Ray, Wright, and Fornander. In neighboring towns, Bohemian (Czech) immigrants such as the Jenik and Jankovsky[263] families farmed or opened businesses to supply the burgeoning farming communities.

The Day the Prairie Dogs Voted

Life "back east" may have seemed a world away. However, by means of the telegraph or the local paper and word of mouth, Chappell residents learned that in the November 1888 election, President Grover Cleveland had been defeated by Republican challenger Benjamin Harrison. Interestingly, Cleveland won the popular vote and Harrison won the electoral vote. Although the Union had been preserved by the Civil War, it was still politically fractured. The vote was still split almost entirely by geography with the Northern states voting Republican and the old Confederate states Democratic. This national political intrigue, however, had nothing on local politics.

Shortly after Joshua's arrival in Nebraska, a brand-new county was formed. In an election held on November 6th, 1888, Deuel County was separated from Cheyenne County. "Chappell, with a large bonfire and two anvils joyfully celebrated the occasion."[264] The new county became official on January 15th, 1889. So, instead of Cheyenne County, the Browns now lived in Deuel County (named for Union Pacific railroad division superintendent Harry Porter Deuel). This set off a bitter and protracted political battle to determine the location of the new county seat. When no town received a majority vote in the first election in January, a second election was held on February 12th, 1889 to make this important decision. The result was one of the most notorious cases of voter fraud in American history. Deuel County District Court records tell the tale. In a judicial opinion dated May 7th, 1894, Presiding Judge Silas A. Holcomb detailed the evidence. In the February 1889 election, the town of Big Springs received 5,608 votes. Chappell received 3,288 votes and the aspiring village of Froid received 292 votes. The problem was obvious: Big Springs and its precinct had no more than 200 legal voters, and Chappell and its precinct had no more than 275 legal voters. Keep in mind, women did not gain the right to vote for another three decades.[265] So, in a county with perhaps 700 legal voters, well over 9,000 ballots were cast! An old wisecrack, well known in the area, explains what happened: all the prairie dogs in the county had voted!

To complicate matters, all the poll books and ballots were stolen or destroyed. Not surprisingly, County Judge Holcomb declared the election "irregular, fraudulent, null and void."[266] Although Joshua had been in the state less than a full year, it can be assumed he eagerly voted in this crucial election—hopefully just once.

The wheels of justice (wagon wheels in this case) turn slowly. When the dust and tumbleweeds finally settled, Chappell was declared the official county seat on June 23rd, 1894. The State of Nebraska continued dividing up the vast western areas into new counties as the population grew. Deuel County eventually lost the northern three fourths of its territory to the newly formed Garden County in 1909.

CHAPTER FOURTEEN

Honor to Pioneers Who Broke the Sods

NEBRASKA HAS ONE OF THE most unique and beautiful state capitol buildings in the country. Located in Lincoln, it rises 419 feet above the plains. As the second tallest state capitol, it can be seen from a considerable distance. An inscription engraved in stone on the north stair buttresses on the outside of the capitol proclaims, "Honor to Pioneers Who Broke the Sods that Men to Come Might Live."[267] One of those pioneers was Joshua Hobbs Brown.

Joshua and Mary's homestead was located north of Chappell on what are known as the "table lands." Their land was three miles north of the Lodgepole Creek and consisted of native prairie covered with grass as far as the eye could see. It was part of what some derisively referred to as the "Great American Desert." The treeless prairie was quite a change from Illinois. In a story passed on through generations, Joshua's and Mary's daughter, Vernice, recounted how her mother cried at simply *seeing* a tree once again after living some time at the homestead. This event happened when the family later visited Ash Hollow, a historic stopping point on the Oregon Trail in the North Platte Valley to the north and east of Chappell.

Yes, life on the semi-arid Nebraska plains was tough. Yet, Joshua and Mary persisted and stayed. Thankfully, the Browns had arrived just months after the deadly "Schoolhouse Blizzard" in January of 1888 where 235 died across the plains, including many children on their way home from country schools. The early years had to have been exhausting. The backbreaking work of "sod busting" (plowing the land to transform the grass-covered prairie to crop-producing farm fields) took years. And working with large horses can be dangerous. In January of 1889, Joshua suffered a severe setback from a farm accident. He was kicked by a horse and left with serious injuries that prevented him from leaving the homestead for several weeks.[268]

Like apocalyptic twins, disease and famine were to follow. In 1889 and 1890 "a diphtheria plague visited the community."[269] It is not known for sure whether Mary was among those contracting this disease. However, in a series of local interest news stories in April of 1890 the *Chappell Register* carried several updates on Mary's health. One story stated, "it is hoped by her many friends that she will continue to improve.[270] One begins to wonder how much hardship one family can endure. But this was just the beginning of their suffering.

Neither the weather nor the economic conditions cooperated with the homesteading effort. A difficult life got even harder. By 1890, Chappell had grown to a population of 250.[271] However, that same year a period of great drought hit Western Nebraska and it persisted for years. Crop failures were the rule in 1893, 1894, and 1895. "The years 1894 and 1895 were the most severe in the county's history. Hot winds seared the already stunted crops. Food became scarce and famine threatened the homesteaders."[272] Things were so desperate that "carloads of food and clothing were shipped from eastern Nebraska to help the western farmers, but many settlers . . . returned east."[273]

At the same time an economic panic swept the state. Many banks failed and farmland became nearly worthless. Hard times lasted from 1890 until at least 1897.[274] The dire situation brought immigration to a halt. Nebraska's statewide population increased only by 7,000 persons between 1890 and 1900.[275] Much of the progress that had been made turning the prairie to farmland in Deuel County had been lost. "The drought of the early nineties, the panic of 1893 and the depression that followed caused vast areas to be deserted."[276] As a result, "Deuel County again became cattle country, composed of small ranches whose stock roamed the open range."[277] Even by 1909, Joshua had only 200 acres of land under cultivation, with much larger tracts of land being used as rangeland for his livestock.[278]

Despite it all, Joshua and Mary somehow managed to survive, and they remained on their homestead.

The Promised Land

When one considers the hardships Joshua and Mary and other pioneer families endured on the windswept and often drought-stricken prairie of Western Nebraska after their long journey from the east, a scene from a much earlier journey to another Promised Land comes to mind: "In the desert the whole community grumbled against Moses and Aaron. The Israelites said to them, 'If only we had died by the Lord's hand in Egypt! There we . . . ate all the food we wanted, but you have brought us out in this desert to starve this entire assembly to death.'"[279] Joshua must have wondered numerous times why he brought Mary and his children to perish in the desert!

The hardships faced by Joshua and other homesteaders can hardly be overstated. But often overlooked or minimized in an attempt to describe what they endured are the reasons the pioneers came to what they too saw as the promised land, and the reasons they stayed in spite of the overwhelming odds. Anyone who has heard the soul-calming song of the meadowlark while it perches on a fencepost early on a bright prairie morning may understand just a little. It's no wonder the Western Meadowlark was chosen as Nebraska's state bird in 1929. But beyond such simple pleasures of life on the plains, there was a far more profound reason they stayed. Those who know the deep-seated pride of farming their own land may understand more fully. When Joshua moved his family west to the frontier of civilization, America was still largely an agrarian society. The land back in Illinois was all settled and spoken for. He and Mary had dreams for their children to farm on land of their own. They had dreams of experiencing the freedom and hope of a new land. This was all possible in the West and they made it happen. Yes, this was home, and it held the promise of a bright future.

Perhaps fittingly, and even symbolically, in hindsight, Joshua and Mary's final child, Benjamin Franklin (Ben) had been born in their new home state of Nebraska on December 11th, 1889. Joshua and Mary's most important and most abiding "crop" was their children. They now had a native Nebraska Cornhusker. He was named, of course, after Joshua's pioneer father. And as it turned out, Joshua and Mary would not be the only Nebraska homesteaders in their family. As their older sons became young men, Cy, Gus, and Joshua Logan, each took out a homestead claim of their own on the prairie surrounding Chappell and joined in the ongoing effort to turn the "Great American Desert" into productive land.[280] As the inscription on the Nebraska Capitol says, "Honor to Pioneers Who Broke the Sods that Men to Come Might Live!"

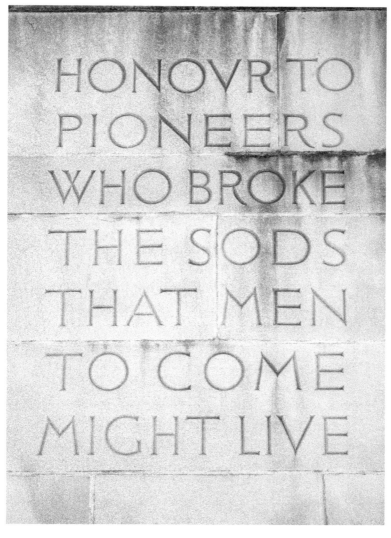

Inscription on Nebraska State Capitol. Hartley Burr Alexander.
Photo by Jerrold Warren Photography.

CHAPTER FIFTEEN
Life on the Plains

JOSHUA AND HIS FAMILY LIVED their lives immersed in nature, the weather, and the rhythm of the seasons. There are four well-defined seasons on the high plains of Nebraska. With annual precipitation at less than 19 inches, the area receives only half the national average. However, significant moisture is received in the spring and early summer, making farming surprisingly productive. About 31 inches of snow fall each winter. The weather is unpredictable, and the daily temperatures range from extreme hot to extreme cold. Average July high temperatures are 90 degrees and average January lows are only 14 degrees. Locals are fond of repeating the saying (sometimes attributed to Mark Twain), "if you don't like the weather, wait five minutes." The climate does have its advantages, though. One reason Joshua chose to make the journey from Illinois was the health benefits of the drier climate. The old cowboy folk ballad *"Home on the Range"* includes the line *"Oh give me a home where the buffalo roam and the skies are not cloudy all day."* Indeed, Joshua and his family enjoyed many sunny days with spirit-lifting blue skies. The semi-arid climate in the Nebraska panhandle produces lots of sunny days—226 per year. Unlike further east, the low humidity and fewer clouds make even many winter days sunny and pleasant.

Regardless of the time of year, Joshua and his family had 360-degree views of the horizon that most people today can only imagine. Unobstructed views of bright sunrises and brilliant sunsets fit for calendars and photo galleries were a daily occurrence. The prairie sky was like an immense, almost endless, canvass of God's artistic creation and luminous color each evening. The dark and crystal-clear night skies revealed countess stars, constellations, and breathtaking views of the Milky Way galaxy. It was truly a scene from scripture: "The heavens proclaim the glory of God, and the sky above proclaims his handiwork."[281] Only the lonely howls of coyotes and the rhythmic chirping of crickets or the wind rustling the prairie grass disturbed the peaceful nights.

After each long winter, springtime was eagerly awaited. Spring does not come early or predictably, though, at 3,700 feet above sea level. The change of seasons in Western Nebraska, particularly in March, brings high winds and, when accompanied by snow, dangerous blizzards. Beginning in late February and peaking in March, the annual spring bird migration presents a true spectacle of nature in Nebraska. Countless thousands of waterfowl and other birds representing multiple species of geese, ducks, Sandhill Cranes, and other birds fill the skies as they journey back north through the Central Flyway. Joshua would also have been an observer of a natural phenomenon now lost and largely forgotten. When he arrived in Nebraska, vast flocks of Eskimo curlews, sometimes covering acres of land, migrated annually across the prairies. This grassland bird has not been sighted in many years and may be extinct.

Beyond nature's spectacle, spring was also a time of anticipation, planning, and hope for the new crop year. In Western Nebraska, the calving season is normally in the spring, with newborn calves appearing from February through March and into April. This requires someone to check on the expectant cows every few hours—day and night. Joshua and his sons spent many hours tending to their herd to ensure survival not only of the calves but also their own family.

With no natural source of surface water on the homestead, the cattle, like the family, initially relied on the Lodgepole Creek or water hauled from distant wells. The long term sustainability of the homestead depended on Joshua finding water beneath the ground. Less than two years after his arrival, in March of 1890, Joshua "found an abundance of water at a depth of 167 feet."[282] Within weeks, Joshua was constructing a windmill tower.[283] No longer would the family need to fill barrels or make trips to the Lodgepole Creek.

Survival required ingenuity and diversification. By the fall of 1890 Joshua had established a small dairy supported by seven or eight milk cows.[284] Feeding a large family required a dependable source of meat, so Joshua also started a swine herd. Almost humorous sounding today, the local paper reported in early 1890 that "J.H. Brown received a fine blooded hog last week, which was shipped to him."[285]

The grazing season for livestock on the upland mixed and short grass prairies does not generally begin until late May because the native warm season grasses like buffalo grass and blue grama lie dormant until then. Before the cows and calves are turned out to summer pasture, the annual rite of branding day occurs. This was an "all-hands-on-deck" undertaking, and often involved the neighboring ranches as well, who would alternate helping each other complete the job.

Branding day began early in the morning with the roundup. Riders on horseback would gather the cows and calves into pens or enclosures to allow for sorting and easier access to the calves for branding, castration, and dehorning. Two mounted ropers, one for the front end and one for the back legs, would pursue and rope the young but growing calves. Once lassoed, a team of two calf wrestlers or "rastlers" (not to be confused with rustlers— who might be hanged!) would grab onto the roped calf and flip it on its right side (since Joshua's brand was placed on the left hip). They then held onto the calf as it was branded with a hot iron and its ears were cropped. Young bulls were castrated and, if necessary, the calves were dehorned. When the job was completed, the rope was removed, and the calf freed to rejoin its loudly lowing mother. Noontime on branding day meant a large feast prepared for all those in attendance. With family and neighbors, and perhaps a few curious guests, the branding dinner was quite an affair. The days following undoubtedly included "rocky mountain oyster" dinners, as there was no electricity or modern refrigeration to preserve this "delicacy" of ranch country.

The September 14th, 1905, issue of the *Chappell Register* included a full page spread of area cattle brands that described how each ranch's livestock could be identified by their unique brand and ear markings. This was a matter of considerable importance at a time when the open range was still transitioning to fenced pastures.[286] Joshua's brand consisted of a cleverly designed combination of his initials, JHB.

Joshua H. Brown's cattle brand. *Chappell Register*, September 14, 1905.
Photo by Steve Grasz

Early summer is a particularly lush time of year on the plains. There is plenty of natural beauty for those who seek it. After June rains, the Brown children would have seen brilliantly colored violet-blue Narrowleaf Penstemon ("bluebells"), the bold cream-white blooms of the yucca plant, and many other flowering native plants. Mary no doubt was presented "bouquets" of prairie flowers by daughters Vinnie and Vernice.

About six weeks after branding day, in early July, the wheat crop would be ready for harvest. "Amber waves of grain" was the goal—acres of ripened wheat like a golden sea rippling in the breeze. Wheat harvesting meant long days in the hot sun, and unlike today, most of it was manual labor. Through the years Joshua saw the area he had chosen to homestead turn into one of the premier areas for hard red winter wheat production in the entire world.[287]

Summer also brought another kind of threatening weather. Thunderstorms on the high plains can be truly frightening and violent with high winds, intense lightning, and booming thunder. They come rolling across the prairie from west to east, leaving either much needed rain or disastrous hailstones, and often both. From the Brown homestead, isolated thunderheads with illuminating flashes of lightning could be seen at night many miles away making their journey eastward across the plains.

Today when travelers drive across the Midwest, they may see endless miles of a single crop. In contrast, farming in those early years was not a wheat or corn monoculture. Surviving and feeding a family required a diverse production. So, besides wheat, Joshua had corn, oats and several other crops as well. Early October was a busy time for harvesting crops, including potatoes. One interesting crop Joshua planted was cane sorghum. In October of 1889, Joshua realized 100 gallons of syrup from his cane crop.[288] If sufficient summer rains fell, the "dryland" corn would also be ready for harvest in the late fall. Irrigation was still unknown on the tablelands away from the Lodgepole Valley.

The obligations of his tree claim meant Joshua and family also spent time planting and cultivating trees. The April 17th, 1890 *Chappell Register* reported that "Josh Brown has a fair stand of trees on his tree claim but will fill in with several thousand more." Arbor Day, which originated in Nebraska in April of 1872, was observed by Joshua with much hope and a few callouses.

In addition to the farming, life on the homestead came with a relentless series of daily tasks and chores. This included tending the vegetable garden, baking bread, feeding the livestock, mending clothes, butchering chickens and hogs, making sausage, preserving food for the winter, milking cows, hand churning butter, and shelling corn, just to name a few. There was little time for leisure, but a special time of year for all the farm families was the Deuel County Fair. During all of Joshua's time on the homestead, the fair was in Big Springs, as it was held there from the county's inception until the early 1930s when it moved to the county seat.

Gentle Giants

When Joshua, Mary, and their children first arrived in Chappell in 1888, a small crowd no doubt gathered at the train depot to gawk—but not necessarily at the new homesteaders. Rather, they stared at what else got off the train—giant beasts the likes of which had not been seen before in those parts. Oral histories can reveal special points of pride in families. For generations, Joshua's descendants passed down the story of how he brought the first Clydesdale horses to what would become Deuel County. Clydesdales are enormous. Standing six feet tall[289] and weighing over a ton[290] (as much as a Volkswagen Beetle automobile) they are an imposing sight. Even a new foal weighs 110-180 pounds, the size of a full-grown person! Fortunately, their size conceals a calm demeanor, earning them the name "gentle giants." To onlookers, their arrival would have been something akin to seeing the arrival of the first tractor. Not only were Clydesdales new to Deuel County, but they were still relatively new and rare in America, having arrived in the 1870s.[291]

Clydesdales are usually bay or dark brown in color with white markings (often white legs, feet, and blazes). They are characterized by feather (long hair) on their legs.[292] Their regal appearance is further highlighted by their high leg movement while trotting or walking.[293] To get an idea of their size, their "shoes" are four times larger than those of thoroughbred horses— about the size of a frying pan or dinner plate.[294]

On Joshua's homestead these giants were used to plow fields and pull farm wagons. All this "horsepower" came at some cost. Adult Clydesdales consume 25-50 pounds of hay and 2-10 pounds of grain each day! Feeding these beasts was not the only chore Joshua and his family had to do to care for them. Their coats, manes, and leg hair had to be brushed clean and their plate-size hooves had to be trimmed and shod with horseshoes weighing five pounds each. Their leather harnesses had to be cleaned and oiled. When the day's field work was done, the Clydesdales had to be cooled down, brushed, and watered before the family could rest or eat. The horses' well-being came first, since the health and soundness of the horses was essential to the Brown family's own survival.

CHAPTER SIXTEEN

"Proving up" the Homestead Claim

HOMESTEADERS LIKE JOSHUA FACED SEVERAL official hurdles and requirements for obtaining title to their homestead land. This generally included living on the land for at least five years, cultivating and improving the land, building a dwelling and, in the case of tree claims, planting thousands of trees. When these conditions were met, Joshua then had to comply with several legal requirements to obtain a "patent." This process was called "proving up" on a claim.

Homestead Act claims, as well as "tree claims," were administered through the United States Land Office at regional locations. The land office for the southern panhandle of Nebraska was located 30 miles west of Joshua's homestead, in Sidney. Since August of 1887, the Sidney Land Office had been located on the first floor of the Tyrone building, a historic two-story limestone structure on the east side of Tenth Avenue.[295]

The legal requirements, of course, were nothing compared to the obstacles posed by the weather. In fact, only about half of all homesteaders successfully "proved up" their claims.[296] Although the reason for the delay is not known, Joshua did not complete the process until 1895, even though the family had lived on the homestead since April of 1888. Given the historic drought from 1893 to 1895 and the simultaneous economic depression, it can be guessed the family may not have wanted to spend money for the necessary fees plus the cost of printing official notices.

The law required that a notice of intent to make final proof in support of a claim be published in the local paper six consecutive weeks. Proof of Publication for Joshua's Homestead Act claim was issued by the *Chappell*

Register on March 6th, 1895, showing that publication of intent to make final proof in support of the claim was published from January 24th, 1895 to February 28th, 1895. The law also required that Joshua make final proof of his fulfilment of the claim conditions before the county judge. This process included witnesses. Final proof to establish Joshua's homestead claim was made before the County Judge of Deuel County, Isaac Woolf, on March 6th, 1895 in Chappell. The witnesses Joshua selected to support his claim were John B. Laycock, Frank Smith, Abraham Stutzman, and William H. Babcock, all of Chappell.

Joshua's witnesses were quite an interesting group. John Laycock founded and operated the "Chappell House" hotel. Frank Smith was the Superintendent of Schools. Abraham Stutzman was a local Mennonite farmer and nurseryman. W.H. Babcock was the town doctor. Perhaps more importantly, from Joshua's perspective, Dr. Babcock was a fellow Civil War veteran, having served in the 95th Illinois Infantry from 1862 to 1865. Likewise, John Laycock served in the 7th Pennsylvania Infantry from 1861 to 1865 and was a prisoner of war for ten months. These men were almost certainly Joshua's friends from the local Grand Army of the Republic (G.A.R.) veterans' group.

After this court proceeding, Joshua paid an $8.00 fee plus a 90-cent testimony fee to the Receiver's Office in Sidney, Nebraska on March 7th, 1895. That same day, he was issued a final certificate (Homestead Certificate No. 2426). The government then approved the claim on May 22nd, 1895 and issued the patent to Joshua on July 8th, 1895.[297]

Joshua's separate "tree claim," which had been made under the Timber Culture Act of 1873, was proved up four years later. It contained 160 acres. The Patent was issued on May 22nd, 1899 through the Land Office in Sidney.[298]

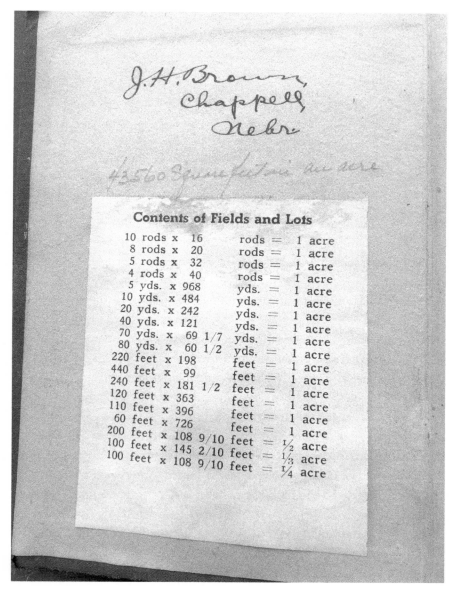

CHAPTER SEVENTEEN
A Legacy of Patriotism and Service

JOSHUA MAY HAVE STARTED HIS Nebraska homestead rather late in life and in hard times, but it prospered in later years. A history of Western Nebraska published well over 100 years ago describes Joshua as "a prominent resident and old timer of Deuel county . . . where he has a very extensive ranch and pleasant surroundings." The same history notes he "is the proprietor of eleven hundred and twenty acres" with "two hundred acres under cultivation." He owned 100 head of cattle plus horses and mules. Joshua was no land baron but was considered prosperous for his area. "He is one of the wealthy men of his region, and highly esteemed as a friend and neighbor."[299] The biographical account ends by stating, "He has built up a fine home and ranch from the wild prairie land."[300]

Not surprisingly, since he was a Union Army veteran, Joshua was described in this history of Western Nebraska as "a staunch Republican." As such, he would no doubt have been pleased to know his original homestead land was later owned and farmed by Haven and Virginia Smith.[301] Virginia represented Nebraska in the United States House of Representatives from 1975 to 1991, and was a legend in Nebraska politics. She was the state's first woman elected to Congress and rose to be the Ranking Republican member on the House Agriculture Appropriations Subcommittee. [302]

Papa Brown

In his later years, Joshua was known around the Chappell community as "Papa Brown." This endearing moniker reveals yet another reason he was such a remarkable man. Joshua and Mary's marriage lasted for 61 years! They raised six children who were productive citizens and notable in their own right.

For pioneers with limited schooling, Joshua and Mary were nonetheless big advocates of education. This was at least in part a legacy passed on by Joshua's parents. When Joshua and Mary were homesteading, qualified teachers were scarce in Western Nebraska and young people with a high school education, and sometimes less, often taught classes.[303] Consequently, most of Joshua and Mary's children taught at some point in the Deuel County schools. Vinnie was held in high regard as a teacher. One news article boasted that "Among the leading events the past week was the closing exercises of Miss Vinnie Brown's school last Saturday afternoon."[304] Surprising, for the time, was the Browns' emphasis on education for their daughters and even college for two sons.

When one considers that Joshua, like his father before him, was born in a log cabin, it is truly amazing—and an American success story—how his family prospered. Joshua's children received more and better educational opportunities than he and Mary could have dreamed possible. This alone made their journey to the West worth all the hardship and toil. Daughter Vinnie, the respected schoolteacher, married Austin Bradley and moved to Peabody, Kansas. They had two children, Max and Marion.

Son Cy was a dispatcher for the railroad in his youth. In 1917, he married Dora Wolf, who had the distinction of being the first child born in Chappell (at her birth on January 10th, 1881, the town consisted only of the railroad section house and one shack). Tragically, Dora fell victim to the global influenza pandemic and died of complications in 1920. A widower after only three short years with Dora, Cy continued farming southeast of Chappell but never remarried. He was among the earlier farmers in the area to engage in irrigated farming. As of 1921, Cy held two surface water irrigation rights on the Lodgepole Creek, via the Soderquist Canal, with priority dates of 1912 and 1915, respectively.[305]

Son Gus attended Wallace Business College in Denver and married Retta Florence Hooper on December 23rd, 1906. Retta was a remarkable woman. She attended Northwestern University before graduating from the University of Nebraska. She later served as the elected superintendent of schools in Deuel County from 1913 to 1922.[306] Her hobby was astronomy. Gus farmed and operated the Brown Lodge Dairy along the Lodgepole

Creek southeast of Chappell. He also delivered milk to customers in town.[307] Gus and Retta's son, Curtis, graduated from Northwestern University and received a master's degree from M.I.T. in electrical engineering.[308]

Son Joshua Logan attended Fremont Normal School and then taught in Deuel County schools from 1903 to 1906.[309] On August 10th, 1910, he married Jennie C. Peterson. They had five children.[310] He became a farmer and stockman near Brule in neighboring Keith County and he served there as a County Commissioner for 20 years. Joshua Logan was also elected to the Nebraska Legislature where he served in Nebraska's unique unicameral as a state senator from 1951 to 1954.[311] His photo can be seen on the first floor of the State Capitol in Lincoln today.[312]

Daughter Vernice attended Deuel County schools in her early years but was sent to live with her sister Vinnie in Peabody, Kansas so she could attend high school—there apparently being no suitable secondary education program established yet in Chappell at this early date. In 1909, at age 21, Vernice married Glenn LaSelle, who later served for over three decades as the elected Deuel County Clerk.[313]

Joshua and Mary's daughter, Vernice, on her wedding day, Chappell, Nebraska, May 12, 1909.

Inspired by her father's military service, Vernice became state president of the American Legion Auxiliary and also its National Committeewoman. She was honored as the very first queen of the Deuel County Fair, in recognition of her community service. Having arrived at her family's Nebraska homestead in a horse-drawn wagon, Vernice lived to see men walk on the moon. She died on February 20th, 1974. Vernice and Glenn's children were Robert LaSelle, a veteran of the European theater in World War II, and Mary LaSelle Jankovsky.[314] Mary graduated from high school in Chappell at age 16 and then attended Chouinard Art Institute in Los Angeles (now the California Institute of the Arts).

Joshua and Mary's youngest son, Ben, was the first of the children to graduate from a four-year university. He graduated from the University of Nebraska College of Agriculture. Ben then farmed south of Chappell before moving to work at the shipyards in Hampton, Virginia.[315]

The community Joshua and Mary helped forge also prospered. Chappell became known as one of the finer small towns in the state. After the turn of the century, and most notably during and after the First World War, the growth of the Chappell community resumed and then accelerated. By 1910, Chappell had a population of 329. In 1911, the impressive residence known today as the Sudman-Nuemann Heritage House was constructed. It became the first home in Chappell with electric lights and running water.[316] In 1915, the current, and still imposing, courthouse building was completed. The following year, the historic Plains Hotel was built. This was followed by the Deuel County State Bank building in 1919. The town was booming. By 1920, the population of Chappell multiplied to 1200.[317] In 1921, the 3,142-mile transcontinental "Lincoln Highway" was completed through Chappell, further connecting the town with the rest of the country.[318]

Deuel County Court House, Chappell, Nebraska.
Photo by Jerrold Warren Photography.

In the years that followed, attractive homes, groomed yards, churches, and well-maintained paved streets made the town stand out. Two municipal parks, a public swimming pool, bowling alley, a 30-acre recreation area and lake, fairgrounds, a beautiful 9-hole golf course and clubhouse, paved airstrip, top-notch high school basketball, football, track and baseball facilities and other amenities made for what Nebraskans like to call the "Good Life." The town also boasts an art gallery displaying works by local as well as world-renowned artists. The gallery, along with the library in which it is housed, were a gift from Orianna Ward Chappell, wife of the town's namesake.[319]

Farming and ranching continue to be the backbone of the economy. Deuel County ranks number four in the state of Nebraska in acres of wheat grown even though the county ranks 82nd in size.[320] Corn is also a major crop—both irrigated and dryland varieties. Other crops include dry edible beans, grain sorghum, millet, sugar beets, sunflowers, and alfalfa. The local farmers cooperative grain elevator grew to one of the largest in the region with the capability of loading large unit trains with wheat or corn. It now has a storage capacity of 5.2 million bushels.[321] Cow-calf operations and cattle feeding are key economic drivers, with cattle still outnumbering people in the county by many multiples. Perhaps due to the toughness and ingenuity needed to thrive there in the early days, Chappell has produced numerous farmers and ranchers who were innovators as well as national and state leaders in the agriculture industry, especially with regard to wheat and cattle.[322]

In addition to its strong farming tradition, Chappell has produced an interesting variety of businesses as well as business and professional leaders. Chappell was the birthplace of Cabela's, one of the world's largest and best-known hunting and fishing outfitters.[323] In addition to the Cabela family, residents have included notable artists,[324] a jazz legend,[325] the "father of the yellow school bus,"[326] and national and state political leaders.[327] The former prairie outpost has also produced prominent surgeons,[328] attorneys,[329] Stanford and West Point graduates, dedicated teachers, pharmacists, nurses, grocers, grain traders, furniture and hardware retailers, agronomists, lumber and seed dealers, dentists, mechanics, petroleum dealers, carpenters, electricians, bankers, realtors, insurance agents, retailers, restauranteurs, and other service providers and business owners. The *Chappell Register* has been published since 1887.

An important component of the town's continued success has been a private foundation, the Thomas D. Buckley Trust. Thomas Buckley (1897-1979) was a local farmer who had started out sod busting. The Buckley Trustees have awarded scholarships and grants totaling $19 million, including $11.5 million in Chappell.[330]

Interstate 80, a major coast-to-coast transportation and trucking corridor, was completed across Nebraska in 1974, with an exit at Chappell. Today, travelers from across the country comment on the attractive little town with the enormous (52 feet by 100 feet) American flag proudly painted on the side of the grain elevator. The landmark flag is a reminder of the patriotism of the community where many have served in uniform.[331]

CHAPTER EIGHTEEN

Dusk on the Plains

JOSHUA'S DAYS AS A PIONEER farmer gradually came to an end. In 1913, Joshua and Mary moved from their rural homestead into Chappell. An early photo shows their new "town" home with a windmill and chickens in the yard. According to Joshua's granddaughter, the house was originally built for Joshua and Mary's daughter, Vernice, and her husband, Glenn LaSelle, upon their marriage in 1909.[332] However, the young couple then sold the house to Joshua and Mary so they could retire from the farm.

During the ensuing years, World War I was fought from 1914 to 1918, and two family members perished from the influenza pandemic of 1918-19. It was also while living in this house that Mary first gained the right to vote, in 1920. That year, Warren G. Harding, the Republican candidate for president, won in a landslide. The stately house still stands on Babcock Avenue in Chappell next to the former Methodist Church parsonage. Joshua's signature, with the date 1922 (apparently when the sidewalk was added), remains clearly visible in the front walkway there today.

Joshua Brown's signature in the sidewalk of his Chappell home.
Photo by Steve Grasz

Joshua and Mary Brown's home in Chappell, Nebraska from 1913 to 1928.
Photo by Steve Grasz

Joshua Brown prominently featured at a G.A.R. Civil
War veteran's convention in San Francisco.

Joshua remained active for many years in Grand Army of the Republic "encampments" or Civil War veterans' reunions around the country. His war service and heroic battle experiences were not forgotten. One postcard from a G.A.R. convention shows Joshua, his beard now white with age, prominently seated on a large flatbed truck during a Civil War veterans' gathering in San Francisco.

Joshua Brown (second from right of flag) at the G.A.R. Civil
War veterans encampment, Scottsbluff, Nebraska, 1925,
commemorating the 60th anniversary of the end of the war.

A History of Western Nebraska written in 1921 recorded that Joshua
was at that time the Quarter Master and Patriotic Instructor of the Crocker
Post, No. 218, Department of Nebraska of the G.A.R. in Chappell.[333] The
G.A.R. was responsible for instituting May 30th as "Decoration Day" to
decorate the graves of Civil War veterans. Today, this is known as Memorial
Day.[334] In 1925, Joshua attended a G.A.R. encampment in Scottsbluff,
Nebraska to commemorate the 60th anniversary of the end of the Civil War.
He was 84 years old.

The sun was setting on Joshua's life, but what an amazing life it had been. For a second time, Joshua—this time with his wife, Mary—had tamed a wild land. He helped turn the Great American Desert into the breadbasket of the world. To this day, the slogan of their Nebraska town is "Chappell, where wheat is king." For the second time in Joshua's life, a civilization with homes, farms, schools, churches, and businesses was founded from the ground up and brought into being by the hard work and perseverance of determined pioneers.

But now, the years were doing what even civil war and the wild prairies could not. Mary's journey was through. She died on January 25th, 1928 at age 83. The January 26th, 1928 *Chappell Register* carried a front page story of one and a half full columns containing her obituary.[335] Joshua may have been as tough as an Illinois oak, but he never recovered from losing the love of his life, his homesteading partner, and companion of more than six decades. Upon Mary's death, Joshua immediately began declining in health. He moved out of his home and in with his daughter, Vernice, and her husband, Glenn, in Chappell so he could be cared for.

Nearly 66 years had passed since a shot from a Confederate musket rifle almost ended Joshua's life in a Tennessee cottonfield along Stones River. And almost that many years had passed since his army's crushing defeat at Chickamauga and the glorious triumphs to follow at Resaca, Lookout Mountain, Missionary Ridge, Atlanta, Nashville, and other battlefields of the Civil War. Could Joshua still hear the deafening bombardment of Atlanta echoing in his mind? Could he still see the faces of his mortally wounded comrades breathing their last on mountain ridges and in hollows across Dixie?

The years since the war had been filled with so many trials: tuberculosis, diphtheria, and "Spanish Flu" outbreaks; prolonged drought and crop failures; economic panic and depression; farm injuries; blizzards; and endless toil. Yet, they had been good years, too. Mary had been by his side all those decades. They proved up their homestead and tree claims and turned the wild prairie into food-producing farmland. They shared each day with family, and they had seen Vinnie, Cy, Gus, Josh, Vernice, and Ben grow up and begin promising lives of their own. Grandchildren now brought new joy.

The nation, once threatened with permanent division, had become a world power and their new community on the plains was prospering like never before. Innovations in agriculture, medicine, and consumer goods were making daily life easier, safer, and more productive than anyone could have imagined. Tractors were replacing horses on the farm. The number of hours required to produce the same bushels of corn and wheat had decreased dramatically since the 1890s. Mechanical corn shellers replaced hand turned ones, and threshing machines had been introduced to process the wheat crop.[336] Automobiles were replacing buggies for transportation. In Washington, the awe-inspiring Lincoln Memorial had been dedicated, and in Lincoln, Nebraska a skyscraping architectural wonder, the new state capitol building, was under construction. Radios and motion pictures were sweeping the country. It was a time of great hope and excitement for the future.

But "to everything there is a season, . . . [a] time to be born, and a time to die."[337] Without the love of his life, his companion through the tears and triumphs, Joshua had lost the will to march on. He had completed his last campaign and was preparing for the final call to muster out of service to his country. Less than a year after Mary's passing, Joshua Hobbs Brown died on December 22nd, 1928. He was 87 years old.

Joshua had lived a remarkable and heroic life. The Illinois prairie had been turned into a garden. The Union had been saved and millions of enslaved people had been set free. The high plains of Western Nebraska had been transformed into productive farms and ranches. The tip of the corn belt had been extended far to the west. Six children had been raised and educated.

The *Chappell Register* carried Joshua's obituary in a large front-page story of one and a half full columns. It was titled "County Pioneer Called by Death."[338]

> *Joshua H. Brown, Civil War veteran and one of the most widely known and highly respected citizens of the community, died at the home of his daughter, Mrs. G.S. LaSelle, in this city, early Saturday afternoon, December 22nd. Mr. Brown was one of the pioneer residents of the county . . . About a year ago . . . Mrs. Brown his helpmate and constant companion for sixty years, passed away. Her death was a great shock to him, and*

*since that time his health has failed much more rapidly. The
funeral was at the nearby Methodist Church with a flag draped
casket. One song by the funeral quartet was "Tenting on the
Old Camp Ground." [Following the service at the church,] "the
Legion marched to the cemetery, where military honors were
paid the deceased." "[A]s the remains were lowered to their
final resting place, taps were sounded solemnly over the grave
and echoed from the hill top beyond.*

The article mentioned Joshua's participation in G.A.R. encampments
in recent years. His Civil War service was also recounted, including,

*taking part in the battles of Perryville and Stones River and
[he] was through the entire campaign march from Louisville
to Nashville under General Buell, following Bragg's army. . . .
He was wounded in the battle of Stones River but was only
disabled for a short time and did not leave his regiment for
a day. Afterwards he was in the battles of Chickamauga,
Lookout Mountain, Missionary Ridge, through the Atlanta
campaign and the battles of Franklin and Nashville.*

Joshua's grave, marked by a Union Army headstone like the ones at
national battlefield cemeteries, is in the Brown family plot in the Chappell
cemetery, still proudly displaying the markings of the 84th Illinois Infantry
Regiment from the hilltop overlooking the Nebraska prairie.

Another obituary appearing in the *Aledo* (Illinois) *Times Record* bore
the headline "Joshua Brown Once Mercer Sheriff, Dies." The sub-headline
read: "Veteran of Civil War Expires at Daughter's Residence in Chappell,
Nebr., Is Well Known Here." It described him as a "pioneer sheriff" and
detailed his Civil War service including his being seriously wounded at
Stones River.[339]

A follow up tribute in the January 2nd, 1929 *Aledo Times Record* by
C.W. Detwiler, whose father served with Joshua, lauded him as a "brave
and efficient soldier and a dependable citizen" who had volunteered for
service "for the express purpose of helping put down the rebellion." He
noted Joshua was "brought up under vigorous pioneer conditions," and that

"[w]hen he was a boy his people were busy turning the tough prairie grass and timber land of Mercer County into a garden." The writer said Joshua possessed "oak like strength."[340] How true a description.

On a cold winter night in December of 1862, twenty-one-year-old Joshua Hobbs Brown had listened wistfully to combined Union and Confederate bands playing "Home Sweet Home" as he and 80,000 other men prepared for the bloody carnage that would follow at daybreak along Stones River—just as the Emancipation Proclamation took effect to free millions from enslavement. He would be seriously wounded but survive to fight on from Chickamauga and Atlanta to Chattanooga, Franklin, and Nashville.

On a cold December day in 1928, Joshua was laid to rest not far from his beloved Nebraska homestead that he carved out of the wild prairie. Thanks to his sacrifice, the republic he loved and served was still one nation, under God, indivisible.

Joshua Hobbs Brown's grave, Chappell, Nebraska.
Photo by Steve Grasz

EPILOGUE

The legacy of Joshua and Mary Brown as homesteaders and pioneers is one of sacrifice, devotion to family and country, and unwavering belief in a better future for generations to come. Joshua and Mary are gone, and others now work their farm with the same steadfast devotion to the land and hope for the future. No one owns fields or farms or houses forever. They care for the land, improve it, and pass it on—hopefully better than before and with faith in the future. Joshua planted trees and broke the sod so that those to come—we who followed him—might live. He shed his blood both on the battlefield and while toiling in the fields to turn the prairie into the world's breadbasket. Somehow, simple gratitude does not seem enough. Indeed, there is a more fitting response. As Joshua's beloved President urged:

> It is for us the living, rather to be dedicated here to the unfinished work which they who fought . . . have so nobly advanced. It is rather for us to be here dedicated to the great task remaining before us . . . that we here highly resolve that these dead shall not have died in vain—that this nation under God, shall have a new birth of freedom—and that government of the people, by the people, and for the people, shall not perish from the earth.[341]

A well-known battle tune sung by Union troops during the Civil War declared that [abolitionist] "John Brown's body lies a-mouldering in his grave, but his truth is marching on!" Likewise, Joshua Brown's body was laid in his grave on a hilltop overlooking the Nebraska prairie, but his sacrifice and service to our county are still felt in the freedom of our people and the two civilizations he helped forge. Joshua Hobbs Brown was once a soldier and twice a pioneer. He is forever an American hero.

APPENDIX

Battle Hymn of the Republic

The "Battle Hymn of the Republic" was a popular patriotic song among Union troops. Its history is worthy of a book itself. The song is thought to have evolved in 1861 from the more irreverent "John Brown's Song" (also known as "John Brown's Body") which celebrated the bravery and heroics of the famous abolitionist and was sung by Union soldiers to the same tune. Even John Brown's Song had different versions and lyrics. As passed down to this author as a child by family members, a verse from John Brown's Song was simply appended to the Battle Hymn of the Republic: "John Brown's body lies a-mouldering in his grave, John Brown's body lies a-mouldering in his grave, John Brown's body lies a-mouldering in his grave, but his truth is marching on!" This, and each verse, was followed by the well-known "Glory, glory, hallelujah! Glory, glory, hallelujah! Glory, glory, hallelujah! His truth is marching on!"

Here are the lyrics of the "Battle Hymn of the Republic" by Julia Ward Howe as published in February of 1862 in *The Atlantic Monthly*.

Mine eyes have seen the glory of the coming of the Lord:
He is trampling out the vintage where the grapes of wrath are stored;
He hath loosed the fateful lightning of His terrible swift sword:
His truth is marching on.

I have seen Him in the watch-fires of a hundred circling camps,
They have builded Him an altar in the evening dews and damps;
I can read His righteous sentence by the dim and flaring lamps:
His day is marching on.

I have read a fiery gospel writ in burnished rows of steel:
"As ye deal with my contemners, so with you my grace shall deal;
Let the Hero, born of woman, crush the serpent with his heel,
Since God is marching on."

He has sounded forth the trumpet that shall never call retreat;
He is sifting out the hearts of men before His judgment-seat:
Oh, be swift, my soul, to answer Him! be jubilant, my feet!
Our God is marching on.

In the beauty of the lilies Christ was born across the sea,
With a glory in his bosom that transfigures you and me:
As he died to make men holy, let us die to make men free,
While God is marching on.

ABOUT THE AUTHOR

Steve Grasz
Photo by Jerrold Warren Photography.

Steve Grasz is a federal judge on the United States Court of Appeals for the Eighth Circuit. He and his wife, Verlyne, live in Elkhorn, Nebraska. Steve grew up on his family's farm and ranch in the Lodgepole Valley of the Nebraska panhandle near Chappell. He is the son of Jane and the late Jess Grasz, and the great-great grandson of the book's subject, Joshua Hobbs Brown. Prior to his nomination by the President, upon the recommendation of both of Nebraska's U.S. Senators, and his confirmation by the United States Senate to the federal bench, Steve practiced law in Omaha. He also served for nearly 12 years in Nebraska's State Capitol as Chief Deputy Attorney General. He is a graduate of the University of Nebraska-Lincoln (B.S. in Agriculture Honors) and the Nebraska College of Law where he was inducted into the Order of the Coif, served as Executive Editor of the Nebraska Law Review, and received the Roscoe Pound Award for Oral Advocacy. Steve has maintained his ties to the land by planting thousands of conservation trees on historic family property along the Lodgepole Creek in the shadow of the Oregon Trail.

END NOTES

Chapter One: Prairie State Pioneer

1   Psalm 145:4 ESV. Joshua Brown's story is also a story of God's providential workings in the history of our country.

2   Mercer County, Illinois is south of Moline, Illinois and southeast of Iowa City, Iowa.

3   The tribe's name is also spelled "Sac."

4   *History of Mercer County* (Chicago: HH Hill and Company, 1882), 809-811 (article on Benjamin F. Brown).

5   U.S. Census Bureau, Census of 1830.

6   *History of Mercer County*, 809-810.

7   William C. Ives, "Abraham Lincoln in Mercer County, Illinois 1832, 1834, 1858," *Journal of the Illinois State Historical Society* 101, no. 3/4 (2008): 329-347.

8   A sketch of Harison Brown is included in the 1882 *History of Mercer County* at page 627. His signature shows he spelled his name with one "r."

9   *History of Mercer County*, 799. They were married by the Rev. Mr. Gardiner of Galesburg, a Universalist minister. *See also* Col. Wm. A Lorimer, *Historical Encyclopedia of Illinois and History of Mercer County* (Chicago: Munsell Pub. Co., 1903), 638 (history of North Henderson Township noting the first marriage).

10   Their land was located at Southwest Section 6, Northwest Section 7, and the East 1/2 of the Northeast Section 12 in North Henderson Township. The legal description is T13, R1W, SW Sec. 6; NW ¼ Sec. 7; and E1/2 Sec.12.

11   Bill and Kay Meeker, interview by author, North Henderson, Illinois, August 22, 2020. The Meeker family was another pioneer family in Mercer County and were neighbors to the Browns. Today, the land once farmed by Benjamin Brown is gently rolling hills covered in tall corn with a beautiful farmstead leading back to wooded creek bottoms.

12   "Joshua Brown Once Mercer Sheriff, Dies," *Aledo (Illinois) Times Record*, Dec. 1928.

13   *History of Mercer County*, 800; Shirley Nall and Joyce McCan, "Mercer Remembers 1835-1985," *Times Record Co.*, 66 (article on North Henderson Township). The Mann Cemetery, located just east of the site of Benjamin and

Lucinda's farm, is located on land donated by James Mann. The first burial in North Henderson Township was at this cemetery in June of 1836. *History of Mercer County*, 799.

14 "The Original Steel Plow," John Deere, accessed on Nov. 14, 2020, https://www.deere.com./en/our-company/history/.

Chapter Two: The Union in Peril, Lincoln Calls

15 *History of Mercer County*, 799.

16 *History of Mercer County*, 61.

17 *History of Mercer County*, 810.

18 U.S. Constitution, amend. 17. The 17th Amendment, ratified in 1913, provided for popular election of Senators.

19 Samuel W. Brown became an "intimate personal friend" of Lincoln and was appointed by Lincoln to a position in the Vancouver, Territory of Washington Land Office in 1861. Cora M. Chrisman and Benj. A Brown, "The Ancestors of Cora M. Chrisman and Benj. A. Brown" (unpublished manuscript, June 1950) (available at the Mercer County Historical Society in Aledo, Illinois).

20 *History of Mercer County*, 809-10. This residence was still standing proudly overlooking the farm until approximately 2018 when it was lost to a fire.

21 L.A. Simmons, *History of the 84th Reg't Ill. Vols.* (Macomb, Illinois: Hampton Brothers, Publishers, 1866), 5. This historical document is a chronological history kept by a member of the Regiment. It is in the public domain. An original 1866 copy was kept in the author's family for generations.

22 Simmons, 5.

23 Simmons, 5.

24 Simmons, 5.

25 Simmons, 7.

26 Simmons, 7.

27 Simmons, 8.

28 "John W Dilley, Mercer Pioneer Penned His Eventful Life Story Here Published Following His death," *Aledo Times Record*, August 28, 1924.

29 Simmons, 9.

30 Simmons, 10.

31 Simmons, 12.

32 Simmons, 12.

33 Simmons, 12.

Chapter Three: Red Trail in the Snow

[34] "Illinois Regiments in the Battle of Perryville," Illinois USGenweb Project, accessed Nov. 13, 2020, https://civilwar.illinoisgenweb.org/battle3s/perryv.html. (Source: Frederick H. Dyer, *A Compendium of the War of Rebellion* (Des Moines: The Dyer Publishing Company, 1908).

[35] Simmons, 13.

[36] Simmons, 13.

[37] Simmons, 14.

[38] Simmons, 17.

[39] Simmons, 17.

[40] Simmons, 17.

[41] Simmons, 18.

[42] Simmons, 18.

[43] Simmons, 18.

[44] Simmons, 18.

[45] Simmons, 18-19.

[46] "Regimental and Unit Histories," Histories of Illinois Civil War Regiments and Units, accessed Nov. 18, 2020, https://cyberdriveillinois.com./departments/archives/databases/reghist.pdf, 261 (84th Illinois Infantry) (Source: *Report of the Adjutant General of the State of Illinois* (Springfield: Phillips Bros., 1900)).

[47] Simmons, 19.

[48] Simmons, 19.

[49] Simmons, 22.

[50] Simmons, 22.

[51] Simmons, 22.

[52] Simmons, 20.

Chapter Four: Emancipation Vindication

[53] Abraham Lincoln, "Second Inaugural Address" (speech, Washington, D.C, March 4, 1865).

[54] Simmons, 23.

[55] Simmons, 25.

[56] "Illinois Regiments in the Battle of Stones River," Illinois USGenweb Project, accessed Nov. 13, 2020, https://civilwar.illinoisgenweb.org/battles/stoneriv.html. (Source: Frederick H. Dyer, *A Compendium of the War of Rebellion*, (Des Moines: The Dyer Publishing Company, 1908)).

57 Illinois Regiments in the Battle of Stones River.

58 Simmons, 27.

59 Simmons, 27.

60 Simmons, 27.

61 Simmons, 28.

62 Jim Lewis, "The Battle of Stones River," *Blue and Gray* Vol. XXVIII, no. 6, 22.

63 Lewis, 22.

64 Lewis, 22.

65 Lewis, 22.

66 Simmons, 28.

67 Simmons, 28.

68 Simmons, 28.

69 Simmons, 28-29.

70 Simmons, 29.

71 Simmons, 30.

72 Simmons, 30.

73 Simmons, 31.

74 Simmons, 31.

75 Simmons, 31.

76 Simmons, 32.

77 Simmons, 32.

78 Simmons, 32.

79 Simmons, 32.

80 Simmons, 34.

81 Simmons, 34.

82 Simmons, 34.

83 Simmons, 34.

84 Simmons, 35.

85 Simmons, 35.

86 Aaron O'Neil, "Number of Casualties at the Battle of Stones River 1862-1863," Statista, updated October 23, 2020, https://www.statista.com./statistics/1010965/battle-stones-river-casualties-1862-1863/.

87 Geoffrey C. Ward, Kenneth Burns, and Richard Burns, *The Civil War* (New York: Alfred A. Knope, Inc., 1990), 318-19 (quoting Gideon Wells).

88 Simmons, 324.

89 Simmons, 43.

90 Simmons, 38.

91 Simmons, 38.

92 Simmons, 38.

93 John 15:13 (NIV).

94 Simmons, 38.

95   "History of McDonough County, Illinois, 1885," Illinois USGenweb Project, accessed Nov. 13, 2020, https://Mcdonough.illinoisgenweb.org/1885civil84ihistory.html.

96   Simmons, 35.

97   "War in the Southwest Its Events," *New York Times*, Jan. 16, 1863.

98   Peter Cozzens, *No Better Place to Die* (Urbana and Chicago: University of Ill. Press, 1990), x.

99   Cozzens, 207.

100   "Battle of Murfreesboro," *Aledo (Illinois) Weekly Record*, Jan. 13, 1863.

101   "Battle of Murfreesboro," *Aledo Weekly Record*, Jan. 13, 1863.

102   "Our Losses at Murfreesboro," *Aledo Weekly Record*, January 20, 1863. *See also* Simmons, 8 (noting Company H was organized in August of 1862 under Captain John C. Pepper).

103   *Compendium of History Reminiscence & Biography of Western Nebraska* (Chicago: Alden Pub. Co., 1909), 1025. (article on Joshua H. Brown) ("At the Battle of Stones River he received quite a severe wound.").

Chapter Five: Defeat at the River of Death

104   Simmons, 35.

105   Simmons, 36.

106   Simmons, 36.

107   "Illinois Regiments in the Tullahoma Campaign," Illinois USGenweb Project, accessed Nov. 13, 2020, https://civilwarillinoisgenweb.org/battles/tullahom.html. (Source: Frederick H. Dyer, *A Compendium of the War of Rebellion*, (Des Moines: The Dyer Publishing Company, 1908)).

108   Simmons, 69.

109   Simmons, 69.

110   Simmons, 69.

111   Simmons, 79.

112   Simmons, 80.

113   "Illinois Regiments in the Tullahoma Campaign," Illinois USGenweb Project, accessed Nov. 13, 2020, https://civilwarillinoisgenweb.org/battles/tullahom.html. (Source: *Dyers' Compendium*).

114   "Illinois Regiments in the Tullahoma Campaign."

115   Simmons, 82.

116   Simmons, 82.

117   Simmons, 82.

118   Simmons, 91.

119   Simmons, 91.

120   Simmons, 107.

121 Simmons, 108.

122 "Battle of Chickamauga," The HISTORY Channel, updated Aug. 21, 2018, www.history.com/topics/american-civil-war/battle-of-chickamauga.

123 Simmons, 110.

Chapter Six: The Chattanooga Campaign

124 Simmons, 110.

125 Simmons, 120.

126 Simmons, 121.

127 "Illinois Regiments in the Chattanooga Campaign," Illinois USGenweb Project, accessed Nov. 13, 2020, https://civilwar.illinoisgenweb.org/battles/chatt.html. (Source: *Dyer's Compendium*).

128 Simmons, 122.

129 Simmons, 130.

130 Simmons, 134.

131 "Illinois Regiments in the Chattanooga Campaign."

132 "84th Infantry History," in *History of McDonough County, Illinois*, 1885.

133 The List of Pensioners on the Roll, January 1, 1883, reveals that John W. Dilley received a pension of $10 a month starting in February of 1880 due to having developed heart disease as a result of suffering from scurvy during the war. "Mercer County, Illinois 1883 Pensioners on the Roll," Genealogy Trail History Group, accessed Nov. 21, 2020, http://genealogytrails.com./ill/mercer/1883pensioners.html.

134 Simmons, 138.

135 "Winter Encampments," American Battlefield Trust, accessed Nov. 20, 2020, https://www.battlefields.org./learn/articles/winter-encampments.

136 "Winter Encampments," American Battlefield Trust, accessed Nov. 20, 2020, https://www.battlefields.org./learn/articles/winter-encampments.

137 Simmons, 158.

138 Simmons, 141.

139 Simmons, 144.

140 Simmons, 144.

141   "Illinois Regiments in the Atlanta Campaign," Illinois USGenweb Project, accessed Nov. 13, 2020, https://civilwar.illinoisgenweb.org/battles/atlanta.html. (Source: *Dyers Compendium*).

142   "Illinois Regiments in the Combat at Buzzards Roost Gap," Illinois USGenweb Project, accessed Nov. 13, 2020, https://civilwar.illinoisgenweb.org/battles/buzzard.html. (Source: *Dyer's Compendium*).

143   "Illinois Regiments in the Combat at Buzzards Roost Gap."

144   "Illinois Regiments in the Combat at Buzzards Roost Gap."

145   "Illinois Regiments in the Battle of Resaca," Illinois USGenweb Project, accessed Nov. 13, 2020, https://civilwar.illinoisgenweb.org/battles/resaca.html. (Source: *Dyer's Compendium*).

146   Simmons, 175.

147   Simmons, 179-180.

148   "Illinois Regiments in the Atlanta Campaign," Illinois USGenweb Project, accessed Nov. 13, 2020, https://civilwar.illinoisgenweb.org/battles/atlanta.html. (Source: *Dyers Compendium*).

149   "Illinois Regiments at Kenesaw Mountain," Illinois USGenweb Project, accessed Nov. 13, 2020, https://civilwar.illinoisgenweb.org/battles/kenesaw.html. (Source: *Dyer's Compendium*).

150   The name of the river is spelled "Chattahootchie" in the 1866 history of the 84th Regiment.

151   Simmons, 183.

152   Simmons, 183.

153   Simmons, 185.

154   Simmons, 185.

155   Simmons, 185.

156   "Illinois Regiments in the Battle of Peachtree Creek," Illinois USGenweb Project, accessed Nov. 13, 2020, https://civilwar.illinoisgenweb.org/battles/peachtr.html. (Source: *Dyer's Compendium*).

157   "Illinois Regiments in the Battle of Peachtree Creek."

158   Simmons, 189.

159   Simmons, 189.

160   Simmons, 190.

161   Simmons, 195.

162   Simmons, 195.

Chapter Eight: From the Brink of Surrender to Victory: The Battles of Franklin and Nashville

163 Simmons, 205.

164 Simmons, 210.

165 Simmons, 210.

166 "Illinois Regiments in the Battle of Franklin," Illinois USGenweb Project, accessed Nov. 13, 2020, https://civilwar.illinoisgenweb.org/battles/battfran.htn. (Source: *Dyers Compendium*).

167 Simmons, 212-13.

168 Simmons, 213.

169 "Illinois Regiments in the Battle of Nashville," Illinois USGenweb Project, accessed Nov. 13, 2020, https://civilwar.illinoisgenweb.org/battles/nashvill.html. (Source: *Dyers Compendium*).

170 Simmons, 223.

171 Simmons, 224.

172 Simmons, 224.

173 Simmons, 224.

174 "Illinois Regiments in the Battle of Nashville."

175 Simmons, 225.

176 Simmons, 228.

177 Although Dyer's Regimental History lists the starting date as December 17, a first-hand account from Joshua's Company states they left Nashville on December 20. It is possible that parts of the Regiment began the pursuit on different days. "Dyers' Regimental History, 84th Illinois Infantry," Illinois USGenweb Project, accessed Nov. 13, 2020, https://civilwar.illinoisgenweb.org/dyers/084inf.html; John Webster Dilley letter to Mary Dilley, January 1865.

Chapter Nine: Winter in Alabama

178 Simmons, 233.

179 Simmons, 234; John Webster Dilley letter to Mary Dilley, January 1865.

180 Letter of John Webster Dilley to Mary Dilley, January 1865.

181 Letter of John Webster Dilley to Mary Dilley, January 1865.

182 Letter of John Webster Dilley to Mary Dilley, January 1865.

183 John Webster Dilley later served as county clerk, county treasurer, deputy sheriff, supervisor, alderman and mayor pro tem of Aledo, Illinois. "John W. Dilley, Mercer Pioneer," *Aledo Times Record*, Aug. 28, 1924. He died on August 22, 1924, and is buried in the Aledo Cemetery, Lot 168. His tombstone bears the markings of the 84th Illinois Infantry Regiment.

[184] Simmons, 234.

[185] Simmons, 234.

[186] Simmons, 235.

[187] Simmons, 235.

[188] Simmons, 236.

[189] Simmons, 234-35.

Chapter Ten: A Time to Dance and a Time to Mourn

[190] Ecclesiastes 3:1-4 (ASV).

[191] Abraham Lincoln, "Second Inaugural Address," (speech, Washington, D.C, March 4, 1865).

[192] Simmons, 252.

[193] Simmons, 253.

[194] Simmons, 254.

[195] Simmons, 254.

[196] Simmons, 255.

Chapter Eleven: Mustered Out of Service

[197] Simmons, 259.

[198] Simmons, 272.

[199] Simmons, 273-74.

[200] Simmons, 274.

[201] Simmons, 275.

[202] Simmons, 275.

[203] "Dyers' Regimental History, 84th Illinois Infantry," Illinois USGenweb Project, accessed Nov. 13, 2020, https://civilwar.illinoisgenweb.org/dyers/084inf.html.

[204] Simmons, 275.

[205] Simmons, 275.

[206] Simmons, 275.

[207] Simmons, 276.

[208] Simmons, 276-77.

[209] Simmons, 277-78.

Chapter Twelve: Love of a Lady, the Land, and the Law

210   "Civil War Casualties," American Battlefield Trust, accessed Nov. 15, 2020, https://www.battlefields.org/learn/articles/civil-war-casualties.

211   Abraham Lincoln, "Second Inaugural Address," (speech, Washington, D.C, March 4, 1865).

212   Mary's birthday was June 1, 1844. *Compendium of History Reminiscence & Biography of Western Nebraska.* (Chicago: Alden Pub. Co., 1909), 1025. At the time of her marriage to Joshua, her name was Mrs. Mary (Dilley) Rodgers. (Marriage License dated Dec. 31, 1866 from Aledo County Clerk). Mary and her first husband, Nathan Rodgers, were married on December 24, 1862. Nathan G. Rodgers is buried in the Farlow Grove Cemetery in Matherville, Mercer County, Illinois. He died on March 3, 1864 at age 26. It is possible, but not known, whether Nathan died while serving in the Civil War. Given the dates, it is possible, albeit speculation, they married just as Nathan went off to war and they never had a chance to live together. He died about 15 months after their wedding.

213   "On the 1st inst. at the residence of the officiating clergyman, by Rev. Jas. D. Taylor, Mr. Joshua Brown and Mrs. Mary Rodgers, both of Mercer County, Illinois." "Married," *Aledo Weekly Record*, January 9, 1867.

214   "Horrible Indian Massacre," *Aledo Weekly Record*, January 2, 1867.

215   *The History of Mercer County*, 809-11. Today, this land can be located at 283rd Street and 50th Avenue south of Viola, Illinois, along highway 67. The legal description is T13, R2W, SE ¼ of Sec. 10 in Suez Township.

216   "Corn Planting," *Aledo Weekly Record*, May 15, 1867 (reporting that if the rains continued the corn would need to be replanted).

217   *Aledo Weekly Record*, June 5, 1867.

218   *Aledo Weekly Record*, July 6, 1870.

219   *Aledo Weekly Record*, July 6, 1870.

220   *Aledo Weekly Record*, July 6, 1870.

221   *Aledo Weekly Record*, July 6, 1870.

222   *Aledo Weekly Record*, Nov. 9, 1870.

223   *Aledo Weekly Record*, April 18, 1871.

224   *Aledo Weekly Record*, May 31, 1871.

225   *History of Mercer County*, 644. The *Aledo Weekly Record* listed Joshua H. Brown as a candidate for Sheriff of Mercer County as part of the "Republican Ticket" in the October 16, 23, and 30, 1878 editions. Joshua had a small ad promoting his candidacy in the October 30 edition.

226   J.H. Brown (Joshua) received 1172 votes. W.H. Brown received 852 votes and candidate Gregg received 927 votes. "Official Vote of Mercer County," *Aledo Weekly Record*, November 5, 1878.

227 His total pay for the first six months of his term was $902.52, which was $242.52 above his salary. *Aledo Weekly Record,* July 23, 1879.

228 "Joshua Brown Once Mercer Sheriff, Dies," *Aledo Times Record,* December 1928.

229 "Gambling At Our Fair," *Aledo Weekly Record,* September 24, 1879.

230 *Aledo Weekly Record,* November 19, 1879.

231 *Aledo Weekly Record,* November 19, 1879.

232 *Aledo Weekly Record,* November 19, 1879.

233 *Aledo Weekly Record,* October 1, 1879.

234 "From Suez," *Aledo Democrat,* August 12, 1887.

Chapter Thirteen: Home on the Range

235 Benjamin Franklin Brown and Lucinda Mann Brown. Joshua's mother, Lucinda, would live on until February 28, 1903. Benjamin and Lucinda are buried in the Mann Cemetery located near 290th Street and 50th Ave. in Mercer County. (Dates confirmed by author at Mann Cemetery, Aug. 22, 2020).

236 "History of Medicine," NIH U.S. National Library of Medicine, accessed Nov. 17, 2020, nlm.nih.gov.

237 A Brown family history written in 1950, states "He contracted or was threatened with 'consumption' . . . and, as many others in those times did, 'went west' for his health." Cora M. Chrisman and Benj. A Brown, "The Ancestors of Cora M. Chrisman and Benj. A. Brown" (unpublished manuscript, June 1950) (available at the Mercer County Historical Society in Aledo, Illinois).

238 Quit claim deed dated September 14, 1885 (Recorded on August 27, 1886 as No. 18592, book 39, page 232, Mercer County Recorder's Office). Lot number 3 of the east half and the west half of section 6, consisting of 16 acres.

239 Joshua likely filed his homestead claim at the North Platte, Nebraska land office which had opened in 1872. *Deuel County History* (Des Moines: Hansen Printing, Inc., 1984), 4. He completed the paperwork at the Sidney, Nebraska land office which opened in 1887.

240 *Compendium History Reminiscence & Biography of Western Nebraska,* 1025. On November 13, 1885, the local paper reported, "J.H. Brown has returned from Nebraska. We understand he purchased land while there." "Brief Local Matters," *Aledo Democrat,* Nov. 13, 1885.

241 Mark Rydell, "The Cowboys," Warner Bros., 1972 (motion picture).

242 Addison E. Sheldon, *History and Stories of Nebraska* (Lincoln: The University Publishing Co., 1919), 269.

243 A.T. Andreas, "Cheyenne County," in *History of the State of Nebraska* (Chicago: The Western Historical Company, 1882).

244 United States Census Bureau, Census of 1870 and 1880.

245 Named for Union Pacific Railroad official Charles Henry Chappell who oversaw construction in the area.

246 "From Viola," *Aledo Democrat*, February 24, 1888 ("We understand that Mr. J.H. Brown, of Suez, has chartered a car and will load his goods this week for Chappel[l], Neb.").

247 "Burlington Railroad Strike," Encyclopedia.com, updated Nov. 19, 2020, https://www.enclyclopedia.com/history/encyclopedias-almanacs-transcripts-and-maps/burlington-railroad-strike.

248 "Both Sides Resolute," *Aledo Democrat*, March 9, 1888. The strike also caused great inconvenience to another family attempting to settle in the area at the same time. "Fred Grasz was put to considerable inconvenience by the railroad strike. He loaded a car with his household effects and was ready to start for the west Monday, the first day of the strike but didn't get away for a week." "90 Years Ago," *Crete News*, March 1978. Friedrich ("Fred") and Wilhelmina (Minnie) Grasz are the author's paternal great grandparents. Fred's 160 acres of land was located at SW1/4 Sec. 35, T15N, R43W in what was then Deuel County. His warranty deed from the Union Pacific Railroad was dated October 13, 1894. He paid $480 or $3 per acre. His address was listed as Day, Nebraska. Day was a small village that no longer exists.

249 *Aledo Democrat*, March 9, 1888.

250 *Aledo Democrat*, March 9, 1888.

251 Aledo Democrat, March 30, 1888 (indicating the continued presence of the family) ("Miss Vinnie Brown of Suez, visited Miss Statta Maxwell Monday.").

252 The Lodgepole Creek is 278 miles in length. "Lodgepole Creek," Natural Atlas, accessed Nov. 15, 2020, https:Naturalatlas.com/creeks/lodgepole-848463.

253 *Deuel County History*, 17.

254 *Chappell Rustler*, May 12, 1886, 1.

255 The 1886 depot structure is still standing and is in use as the office for the local RV park and campground in Chappell, some 134 years later.

256 "Deuel County, Nebraska," History Nebraska Records: 1874-1975 RG 268, accessed Nov. 18, 2020, https://history.nebraska.gov/sites/history.nebraska.gov/files/doc/Deuel.

257 Elinor Nelson, "Deuel County Who's Who - 1940," NEGenWeb Deuel County, accessed Nov. 15, 2020, www.negenbeb.net, 261-267.

258 Deuel County Who's Who, 263.

259 "Land Grants and the Decline of the Railroads," NET, accessed Nov. 17, 2020, https://www.Nebraskastudies.org/en/1850-1874/railroads-settlement/land-grants-decline-railraods/.

260 *Daily Nebraska State Journal* (Lincoln), June 5, 1887.

261 Paul Kuhlmann, "A Brief History of the Mennonites in Nebraska" Student Work 357, 1953, https://digitalcommons.unomaha.edu/studentwork/357, 13.

262 Glenn S. LaSelle, Joshua's future son-in-law, arrived in Chappell with his parents, Frank and Hattie, in 1900.

263 Adolph Jankovsky, who had been born in Bohemia in 1863, opened a general store in Lodgepole (nine miles west of Chappell) in 1901. In 1906, he moved his business to Sedgewick (14 miles south of Chappell across the Colorado border). This move was prompted by the opening of the area to irrigation from a new reservoir storing water from the South Platte River and the rush of settlement that followed. (Leonard Jankovsky letter to author, July 1987). Adolph's son, Leonard, would marry Joshua's granddaughter, Mary LaSelle. They are the maternal grandparents of the author.

264 Deuel County Who's Who.

265 U.S. Constitution, amend 19. The 19th Amendment became effective in 1920.

266 *Abel V. Carlson et al. vs B.G. Hoover et al.*, Dist. Ct. of Deuel County (April Term 1894).

Chapter Fourteen: "Honor to Pioneers Who Broke the Sods"

267 "Hartley Burr Alexander," Nebraska State Capitol, Nebraska Capitol Commission, accessed Nov. 16, 2020, https://capitol.nebraska.gov/building/history/team/hartley-burr-alexander.

268 *Chappell Register*, Jan. 23, 1889 and February 13, 1890. The *Chappell Register* has been published since 1887.

269 Deuel County Who's Who.

270 *Chappell Register*, April 10, 1890.

271 *Union Pacific Railroad Gazetteer of the State of Nebraska*, 1890 (article on Deuel County), accessed Nov. 17, 2020, https://www.usgennet.org/usa/ne/county/deuel/gazeteer.html.

272 Deuel County Who's Who.

273 Deuel County Who's Who.

274 Addison E. Sheldon, *History and Stories of Nebraska* (Lincoln: The University Publishing Co., 1919), 269.

275 "Drought and Depression in 1890s Nebraska," History Nebraska, accessed, Nov. 16, 2020, https:/history.nebraska.gov/publications/drought-and-depression-189.

276 *Deuel County History*, 5.

277 *Deuel County History*, 5.

278 *Compendium of History Reminiscence & Biography of Western Nebraska*, 1024-1025.

279 Exodus 16: 2-3 (NIV).

280 Cyrus Brown homestead: Patent received March 30, 1895. Doc No. 3384. 6th PM 13N, 44W, NE1/4 Sec. 30; 160 acres; Gus B. Brown homestead: Patent received January 30, 1906; Doc. 3445. 6th PM, 13N, 44W, Sec. 30, Deuel Co., 160 acres; Joshua L. Brown homestead: Patent received June 25, 1908; Doc. 7843. 6th PM, 18N 44W, SE1/2 Sec. 25, Garden County, 160 acres.

Chapter Fifteen: Life on the Plains

281 Psalm 19:1 (ESV).

282 "Local Matters," *Chappell Register*, March 13, 1890.

283 *Chappell Register*, April 3, 1890.

284 "Local Matters," *Chappell Register*, November 6, 1890.

285 *Chappell Register*, January 2, 1890.

286 The *Chappell Register*, September 12, 1889 ("crops on the south divide have been damaged lately by range cattle.").

287 This wheat variety is used to make bread flour and all-purpose flour.

288 *Chappell Register*, October 10, 1889.

289 17-18 hands or 68-72 inches.

290 "Questions," Clydesdale Breeders of the USA, accessed Nov. 16, 2020, https://www.clydesusa.com/faq-687 (1600 to 2400 pounds).

291 "Clydesdale," Homestead on the Range, accessed Nov. 16, 2020, Homesteadontherange.com.

292 "Clydesdale," Britannica, accessed Nov. 16, 2020, https://www.Britannica.com/animal/Clydesdale.

293 "Questions," Clydesdale Breeders of the USA, accessed Nov. 16, 2020, https://www.clydesusa.com/faq-691.

294 "Questions," Clydesdale Breeders of the USA, accessed Nov. 16, 2020, https://www.clydesusa.com/faq-687.

Chapter Sixteen: Proving Up the Homestead Claim

295 The limestone for the Tyrone building was quarried from the Haskell homestead north of Sidney. "Sidney Downtown Historic District," US Dep't of the Interior, Nat. Reg. of Historic Place Continuation Sheet, CN09-074; C.D. and Mercy Essig Building ("Tyrone Building") 1887, Sec. 7, Page 4. Courtesy of the Cheyenne Co. Historical Society.

296 "Homesteading by the Numbers," Homestead National Monument of America, National Park Service, accessed Nov. 16, 2020, https://www.nps.gov/home/learn/historyculture/bynumbers.htm.

297 Joshua's homestead (Homestead Act Application No. 812) was located at E1/2 of NW ¼ and Lots 1 and 2 of Section 18, Township 13N of Range 44W of the 6th PM (13N 44W, E1/2NW1/4, Sec. 18) in Deuel County. It contained 164.61 acres. The homestead was recorded in Vol. 6, page 129, in the Sidney Land Office. Because the claim contained more than the standard 160 acres, Joshua had already paid $11.50 to the Receiver's Office in Sidney, NE on April 7, 1888 for 4.61 acres of land in excess "in said Tract over the area entered under the Homestead Act per application 812." A certificate showing "excess paid at entry" was issued on March 7, 1895.

298 The tree claim was located at NE 6th PM, Township 13N, Range 45W, Sec. 12, Deuel County (SE1/4, Sec. 12, 13N, R45W). Timber Culture Certificate No. 805; Application No. 7792.

Chapter Seventeen: A Legacy of Patriotism and Service

299 *Compendium of History Reminiscence & Biography of Western Nebraska*, 1024-1025.

300 *Compendium of History Reminiscence & Biography of Western Nebraska*, 1024-1025.

301 Part was purchased by Haven Smith in 1933 and part in 1941 (real estate records, Deuel County Clerk).

302 The author worked in Congresswoman Smith's Washington, D.C. office in the mid-1980s. Jack Hart, *Virginia Smith, A Nebraska Treasure* (Lincoln: J & LLee Co., 2003), 30.

303 R. McClaran Sawyer, "No Teacher for the School: The Nebraska Junior Normal School Movement," *Nebraska History* 52 (1971): 190-203.

304 *Chappell Register*, July 24, 1890.

305 "Fourteenth Biennial Report of the Department of Public Works, *1921-1922*," Nebraska Department of Natural Resources, accessed December 17, 2020,

306 Deuel County Who's Who.

307 The author recalls playing frontiersman using what was said to be the old muskrat skin cap Gus had used on cold winter mornings while delivering milk.

308 Gus and Retta moved to Boise, Idaho in their later years to be near Curtis. Gus died in 1968; Retta in 1976.

309 Nellie E. and J.S. Kroh, "Keith County Who's Who – 1940," NEGenWeb Keith County, accessed Dec. 14, 2020, http://sites.rootsweb.com/~nekeith/1040wwbios.html. A "Normal School" was the name for a teacher's college. This is now Midland University in Fremont, Nebraska.

310 Kenneth, Philip, Gerald, Doris and LaVonne.

311 *Nebraska Blue Book*, Nebraska Legislative Council, (Lincoln: Nebraska Legislative Council, 1954), 269.

312 Joshua Logan died in 1957.

313 Glenn served as County Clerk from 1923 to 1956. Glenn's granddaughter, Jane Grasz, would also hold this same office from January 1987 to August 1997.

314 Mary married Leonard Jankovsky and they operated a grocery and dry goods business in nearby Ovid, Colorado for many years. They had two children: Jane and Antonia (Toni). Jane married Jess Grasz and they had three children: Tracy, Steve and Mary. They farmed near Chappell. Toni married Roy Wheeler and they had three children: Robin, Ron and Amy. Toni and Roy live at Sterling, Colorado. Ron farms in the South Platte Valley near Sterling, about 60 miles from Joshua's homestead.

315 Ben had a daughter, Mae, who was placed for adoption with a local family. As an adult, she married Earl Clark of Chappell. Their children and grandchildren were a big part of the Chappell community for decades. Ben married Eunice Lee Lightfoot and they made their home in Newport News, Virginia. They had two daughters, Virginia (Utley) and Laurel (Hays). Virginia lived in Costa Rica in her later years.

316 "Sudman-Neumann Heritage House," City of Chappell, Nebraska, 2020, accessed Nov. 17, 2020, https://www.chappellne.org/heritage-house.

317 *Deuel County History*, 5.

318 Today, this is U.S. Highway 30.

319 "Chappell Memorial Library Dedication," You Tube video, 2:30, July 18, 1936, https://youtu.be/cBgV410CmH8 (featuring Nebraska Governor Leroy Cochron, Chappell Mayor W.E. Zehr and Orianna Ward Chappell (1844-1942)).

320 "2012 Census of Agriculture," Deuel County Nebraska, accessed Nov. 18, 2020, nass.usda.gov.

321 Frenchman Valley Farmers Co-op text to author, September 8, 2020.

322 Merlyn Carlson served as president of the National Cattleman's Association, Director of the Nebraska Department of Agriculture and a Deputy Undersecretary of Agriculture in Washington, D.C. Other area farmers held leadership positions with the Farm Bureau, the Nebraska Cattlemen's Association, and the Nebraska Wheat Growers Association. Carl Bruns served as president of the National Association of Wheat Growers. Larry Flohr served many years on the Nebraska Wheat Board. Charles Fenster was a pioneering university researcher in dryland cropping systems. Billy Ray helped draft the 1980 Federal Crop Insurance Act.

323 Jane Grasz, the author's mother, was perhaps the first worker hired by the fledgling business in 1961. She relates that she typed addresses on envelopes for one cent a piece for Cabela's brand-new mail-order enterprise. She would type late into the night while her children slept, delivering the finished envelopes to

the Cabela's building across the street from the Deuel County Courthouse. Upon her arrival each morning, Richard (Dick) Cabela would throw a rubber ball to distract the aggressive guard dog so she could enter. By 2016, when Cabela's was purchased by Bass Pro Shops, it had nearly 20,000 employees.

[324] Aaron Gunn Pyle (1909-1972). "Facts about Aaron Pyle," askART, accessed Nov. 17, 2020, https://www.askart.com/artist/Aaron_Gunn_Pyle.aspx.

[325] Jack Teagarden (1905-1964) (regarded as the preeminent American jazz trombone player of his time). Michael Palmer, "A Concise Biography of Jack Teagarden," accessed Nov. 14, 2020, https://jackteagarden.info/michael-palmer/biog.htm.

[326] "Frank W. Cyr, 'Father of the Yellow School Bus' Dies at the Age of 95," Columbia University Teachers College, June 28, 2002, tc.columbia.edu. Frank Cyr (1900-1995), a former superintendent of schools in Chappell, was a specialist in rural education.

[327] One is legendary Congresswoman Virginia Smith (1911-2006). Congresswoman Smith is listed number 68 on a list of 150 Notable Nebraskans of all time. "150 Notable Nebraskans," Lincoln Journal Star, Oct. 12, 2020, journalstar.com. Another is Nebraska State Senator Ramey Whitney (1908-1988), who served on the state constitutional revision commission. Stanley M. Talcott, "Amending the Nebraska Constitution in the 1971 Legislature, 50 Neb. L. Rev. 676 (1971), https://digitalcommons.unl.edu/nlr/vol50/iss4/8.

[328] Dr. Daniel (Dan) and Dr. William (Bill) Lydiatt. The Lydiatt brothers are prominent ENT-Otolaryngologists. Bill was the Chief Medical Officer of Methodist Hospital in Omaha as of 2020.

[329] Attorneys in or from Chappell have included E.O. and Bob Richards, Leland Carlson, Dwight Smith, John D. Wertz, John Ross Wertz, John Shunk, Ray Smith and the Honorable Joel Jay.

[330] "Thomas D. Buckley Trust," accessed Nov. 21, 2020, www.thomasbuckleytrust.com.

[331] One resident, Billy Ray, was awarded the Distinguished Flying Cross, the Air Force Medal with 4 Oak Leaf Clusters, the Purple Heart, and the Prisoner of War Medal in WWII. At least 23 Deuel County men lost their lives in war. "U.S. War Casualties Nebraska, Deuel County," Gold Star Casualty Search, accessed Nov. 19, 2020, https://www.honorstates.org/index.php?do=q&state=NE&county=Deuel.

Chapter Eighteen: Dusk on the Plains

[332] The property (Lots 5 and 6 of Block 12) (392 Babcock Avenue) was purchased on February 27, 1909 by Glenn S. LaSelle for $125. A mortgage was recorded to the Chappell Building and Loan Association on March 1, 1911 and released on January 23, 1913. The property was sold by Glenn and Vernice to J.H. Brown on January 23, 1913. (real estate records, Deuel County Clerk).

333 Grant L. Shumway, *History of Western Nebraska and its People* (Lincoln: The Western Publishing and Engraving Company, 1921) (ch. IX, "Deuel County's War Record").

334 The 1921 *History of Western Nebraska and its People* lists the Junior Vice Commander of the Crocker Post as August Guenin. He was known to the Brown children and grandchildren as "Uncle Johnny Guenin." Guenin is buried in the Brown family plot in the Chappell cemetery.

335 "Mrs. J.H. Brown Called To Rest," *Chappell Register*, January 26, 1928, 1.

336 "Farming in the 1920s – Machines – Harvesting Wheat," Wessels Living History Farm, accessed Nov. 16, 2020, https://Livinghistoryfarm.org.

337 Ecclesiastes 3:1-2 (NKJV).

338 "County Pioneer Called by Death," *Chappell Register*, December 27, 1928, 1.

339 "Joshua Brown Once Mercer Sheriff, Dies," *Aledo Times Record*, Dec. 1928.

340 "Late Joshua Brown, Gentleman, Son of Sturdy Pioneers and Good Soldier, Says Aledoan," *Aledo Times Record*, January 2, 1929.

Epilogue

341 Abraham Lincoln, "Gettysburg Address" (speech, Gettysburg, PA, November 19, 1863).

Lightning Source UK Ltd.
Milton Keynes UK
UKHW041839260121
377731UK00008B/531/J

9 781665 512077